The Architectural Plates from the "Encyclopédie"

Edited by

DENIS DIDEROT

DOVER PUBLICATIONS, INC.

NEW YORK

Bibliographical Note

The Architectural Plates from the "Encyclopédie" is a new (1995) Dover selection of illustrations originally published in the *Encyclopédie, ou Dictionnaire Raisonné des Sciences, des Arts, et des Métiers,* Paris, 1751–1780. The introductory Note, captions and Appendix have been specially created for the present edition.

Library of Congress Cataloging-in-Publication Data

The architectural plates from the "Encyclopédie" / edited by Denis Diderot.
    p.   cm. — (Dover pictorial archive series)
    ISBN 0-486-27954-5 (pbk.)
    1. Architecture—Details. 2. Architectural drawing—18th century. 3. Building—Details. 4. Building—History—18th century. 5. Encyclopédie—Illustrations. I. Diderot, Denis, 1713–1784. II. Encyclopédie. Selections. III. Series.
NA2840.A73   1995
720'.22'24409033—dc20
                          95-14027
                          CIP

Manufactured in the United States of America
Dover Publications, Inc., 31 East 2nd Street, Mineola, N.Y. 11501

NOTE

A MILESTONE IN the history of Western thought, *L'Encyclopédie, ou Dictionnaire Raisonné des Sciences, des Arts, et des Métiers* (The Encyclopedia, or Classified Dictionary of Sciences, Arts and Trades) was published in 28 volumes (17 of text, 11 of plates) between 1751 and 1772, with five supplementary volumes (four of text, one of plates) added in 1776–1777 and two index volumes in 1780. Although it was a collaborative effort, with articles written by many leading thinkers of the French Enlightenment (including Voltaire), the *Encyclopédie* in its totality reflected the conception of Denis Diderot (1713–1784), the writer and philosopher who edited the first 28 volumes. Under Diderot's editorship—initially in collaboration with the noted mathematician Jean Le Rond d'Alembert—what had been conceived by the publisher as a French translation of Ephraim Chambers' two-volume English *Cyclopaedia* (1728) was transformed into an entirely new work, which courageously set out to classify and record knowledge in a rational manner, free of political or religious bias.

For many topics, Diderot made use of illustrations to convey information in as concrete and useful a manner as possible (these were published in separate volumes, as noted above). These plates provide particularly detailed and extensive documentation of a wide range of trades, some of which had received little or no attention from previous authors. In addition to the systematic depiction of methods, tools and materials—often from the stage of gathering raw components to the use of them in finished products—the *Encyclopédie* also presented model or idealized forms, evidence of Diderot and his associates' intention to influence the thought and taste of their readers.

This volume contains a selection of illustrations relating to architecture and allied trades from the *Encyclopédie*. These plates have been drawn from relevant subject areas in the volumes edited by Diderot (original spellings): "Architecture" (including the subcategories "Carreleur" [Floor-Tiling], "Couppe des Pierres" [Stonecutting] and "Maçonnerie" [Masonry]), "Charpente" (Wood-Frame Construction), "Couvreur" (Roof-Tiling), "Marbrerie" (Marblework), "Théatres" (Theatres) and "Tuilerie" (Tilemaking). Relevant plates have also been taken from the 1776–1777 supplement ("Architecture" and "Théatres"). The illustrations have been discreetly rearranged for thematic coherence, and a few concerning subjects not relevant to land architecture (such as shipbuilding) have been omitted (a listing of the original subject classifications and positions of the plates is included as an appendix). The captions are new and are merely identifications, not translations of the more detailed original texts.

Readers interested in a broader insight into the scope and background of trades depicted in the *Encyclopédie* are referred to *A Diderot Pictorial Encyclopedia of Trades and Industry: 485 Plates Selected from 'L'Encyclopédie' of Denis Diderot,* edited by Charles C. Gillispie, which includes extensive commentary (available in two volumes from Dover Publications, ISBN 0-486-27428-4 and 0-486-27429-2).

CONTENTS

The Architectural Plates
from the "Encyclopédie"

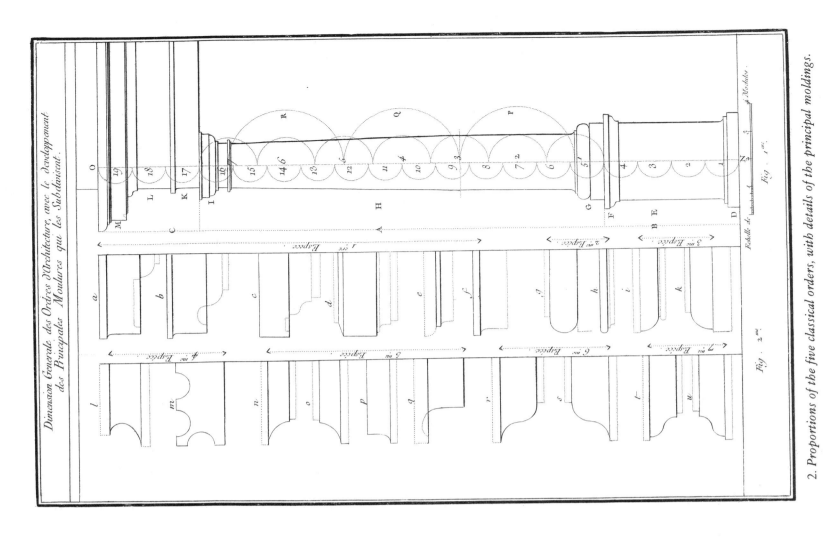

Dimension Générale des Ordres D'Architecture, avec le Développement
des Principales Moulures qui les Subdivisent.

2. Proportions of the five classical orders, with details of the principal moldings.

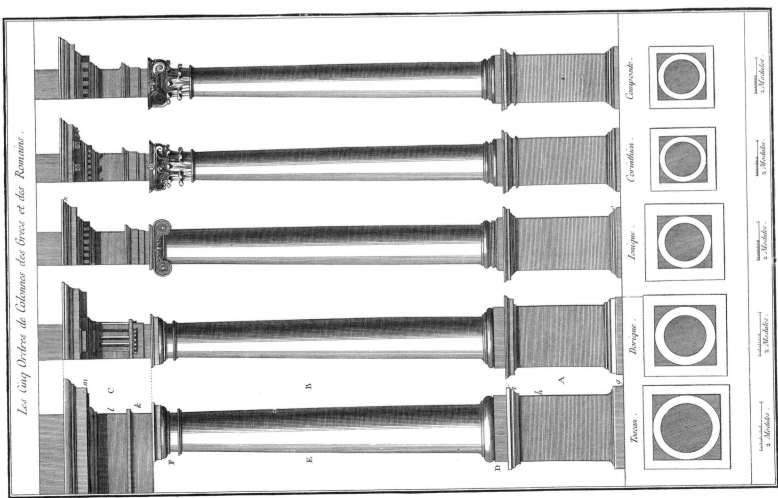

Les Cinq Ordres de Colonnes des Grecs et des Romains.

Toscan.   Dorique.   Ionique.   Corinthien.   Composite.

1. The five classical orders of Greek and Roman architecture.

1

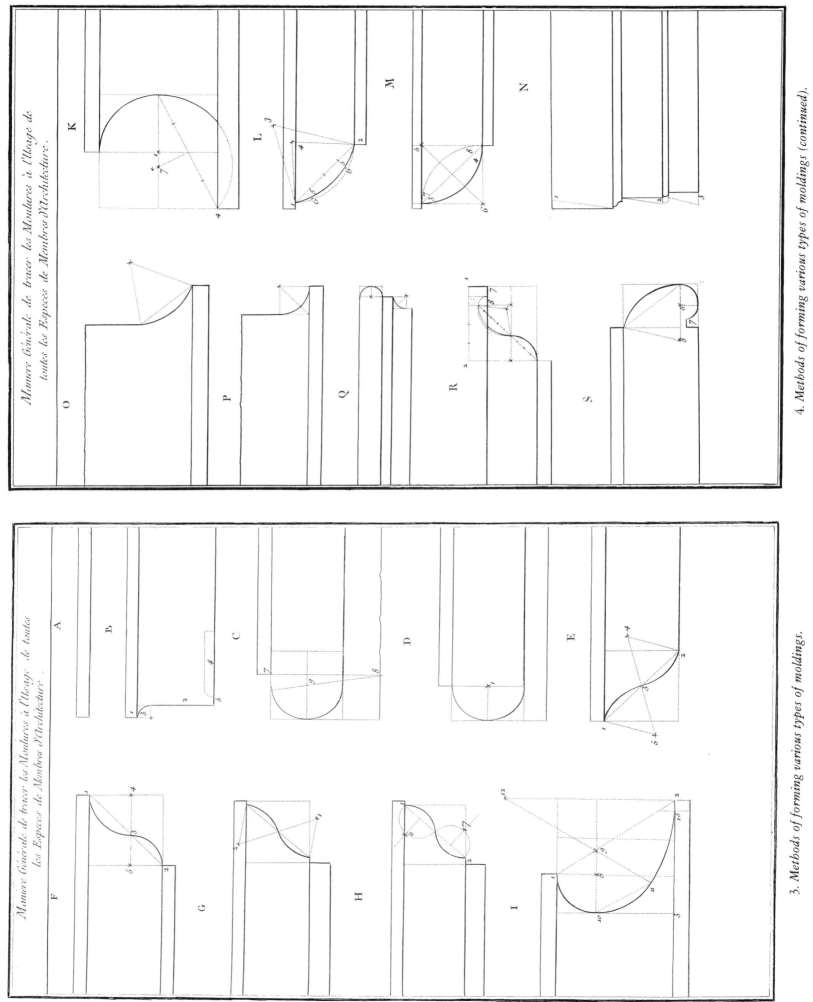

Manière Générale de tracer les Moulures à l'Usage de toutes les Espaces de Membres d'Architecture.

K

L

M

N

O

P

Q

R

S

4. Methods of forming various types of moldings (continued).

Manière Générale de tracer les Moulures à l'Usage de toutes les Espaces de Membres d'Architecture.

A

B

C

D

E

F

G

H

I

3. Methods of forming various types of moldings.

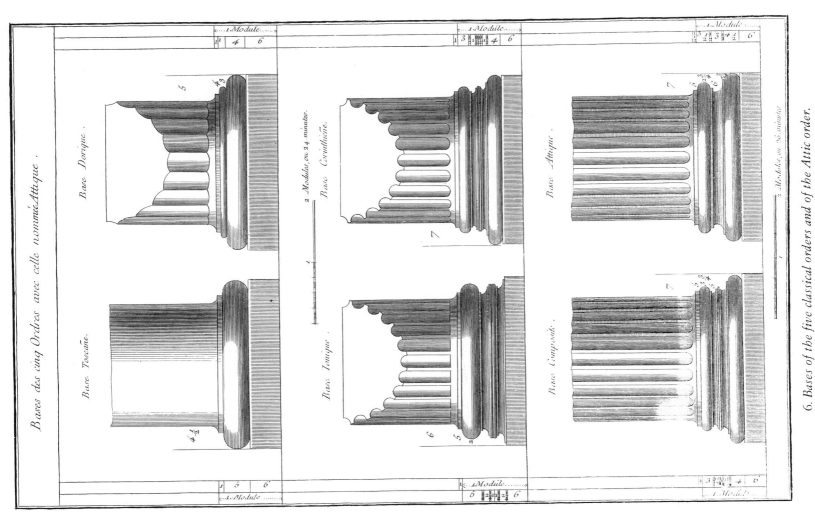

Bases des cinq Ordres avec celle nommée Attique.

Base Dorique.

Base Toscane.

Base Corinthienne.

Base Ionique.

Base Attique.

Base Composite.

6. Bases of the five classical orders and of the Attic order.

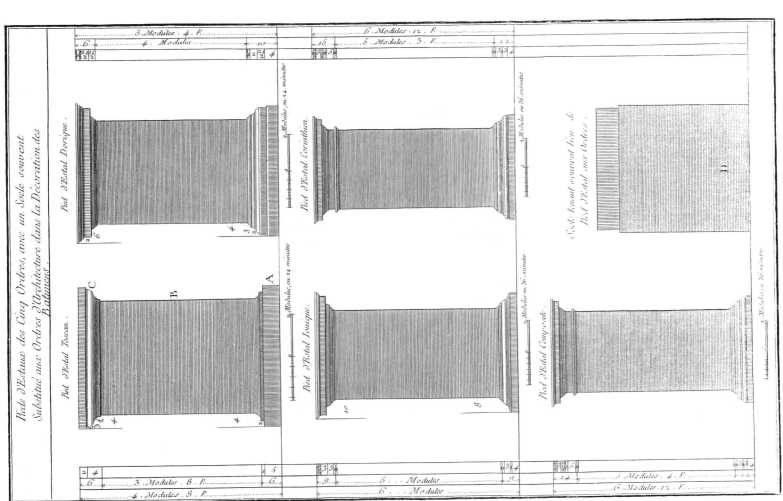

Pieds d'Estaux des Cinq Ordres, avec un Socle souvent Substitué aux Ordres d'Architecture dans la Décoration des Bâtimens.

Pied d'Estal Dorique.

Pied d'Estal Toscan.

Pied d'Estal Corinthien.

Pied d'Estal Ionique.

Socle tenant souvent lieu de Pied d'Estal aux Ordres.

Pied d'Estal Composite.

5. Pedestals of the five classical orders, with a stand frequently used in their place.

3

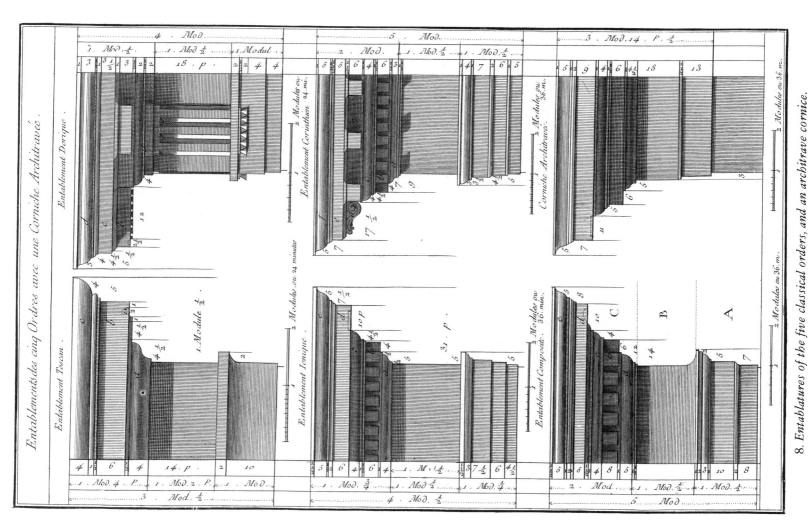

8. Entablatures of the five classical orders, and an architrave cornice.

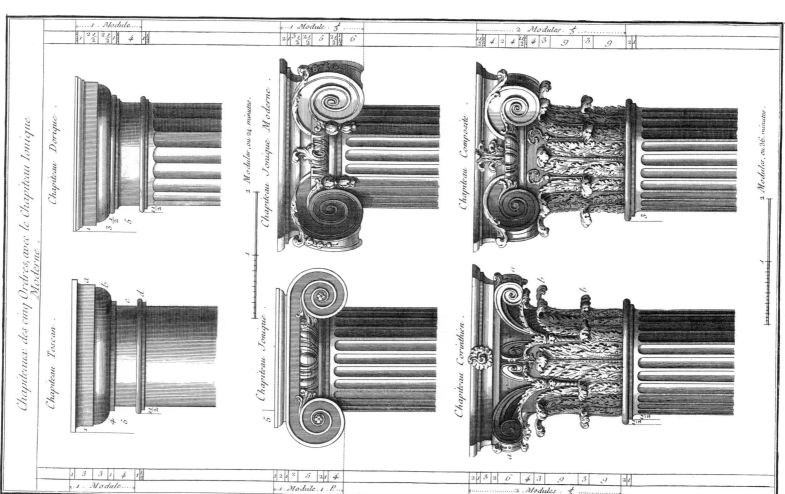

7. Capitals of the five classical orders and of the Modern Ionic order.

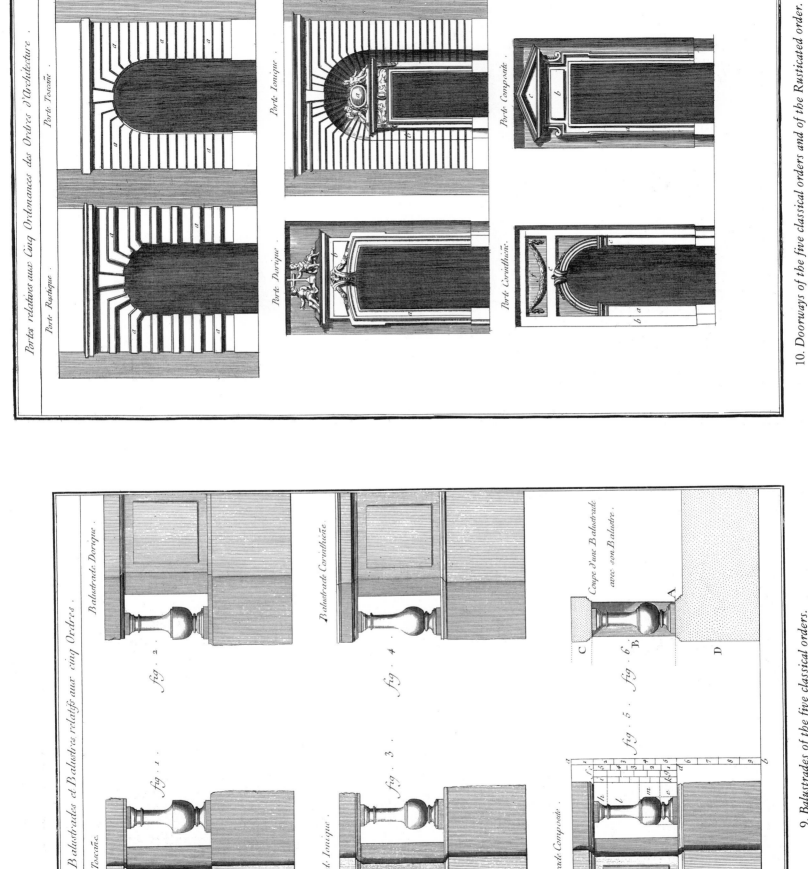

Portes relatives aux Cinq Ordonances des Ordres d'Architecture .

Porte Toscane .

Porte Rustique .

Porte Ionique .

Porte Dorique .

Porte Composite .

Porte Corinthien .

10. Doorways of the five classical orders and of the Rusticated order.

Balustrades et Balustres relatifs aux cinq Ordres .

Balustrade Dorique .

Balustrade Toscane .

fig . 1 .

fig . 2 .

Balustrade Corinthiene .

Balustrade Ionique .

fig . 3 .

fig . 4 .

Coupe d'une Balustrade avec son Balustre .

Balustrade Composite .

fig . 5 .

fig . 6 .

9. Balustrades of the five classical orders.

5

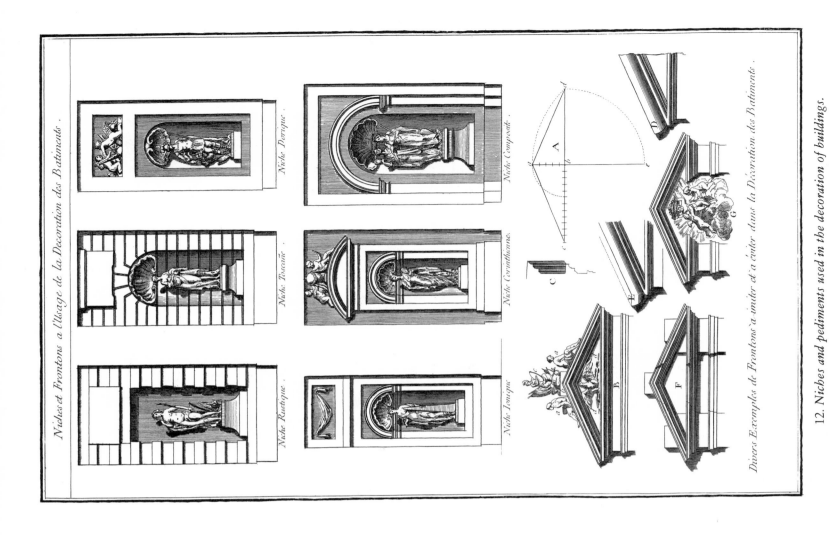

Niches et Frontons à l'Usage de la Decoration des Batimens.

Niche Dorique.

Niche Composite.

Niche Toscane.

Niche Corinthienne.

Niche Rustique.

Niche Ionique.

Divers Exemples de Frontons à imiter et à éviter dans la Décoration des Batimens.

12. Niches and pediments used in the decoration of buildings.

Croisées relatives au cinq Ordonances des Ordres d'Architecture.

Croisée Rustique.

Croisée Dorique.

Croisée Corinthienne.

Croisée Toscane.

Croisée Ionique.

Croisée Composite.

11. Casement windows of the five classical orders and of the Rusticated order.

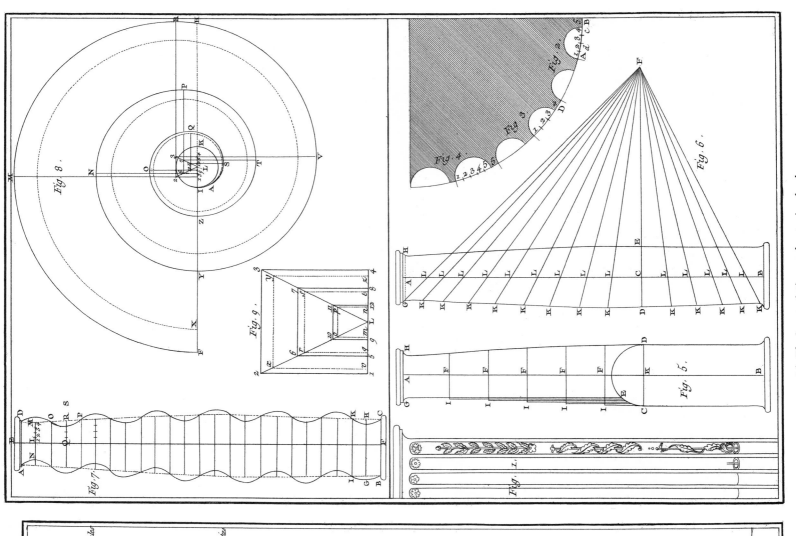

14. *Fluting, twisting and entasis of columns.*

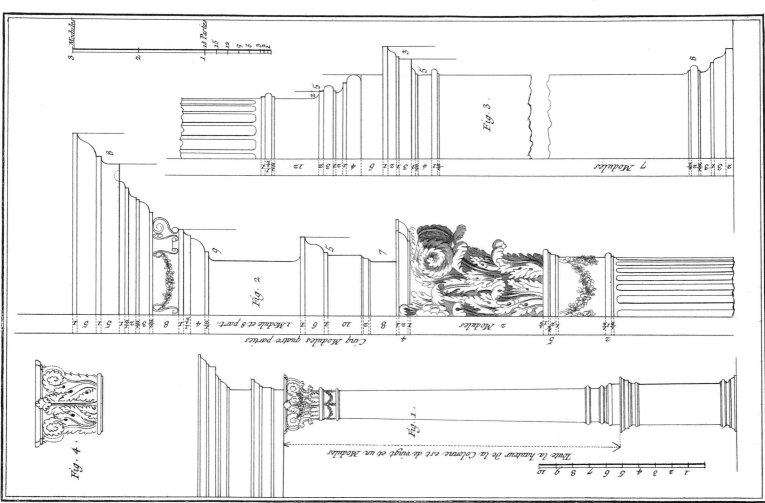

13. *"A new order of architecture."*

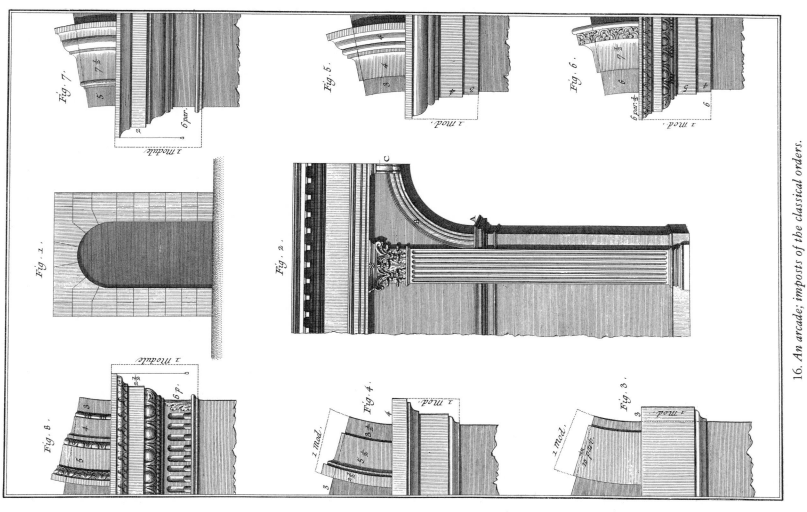

16. *An arcade; imposts of the classical orders.*

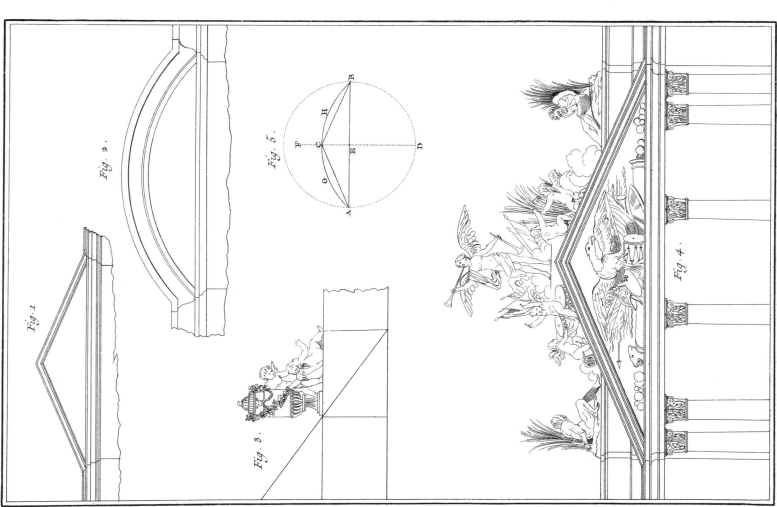

15. *Various pediments.*

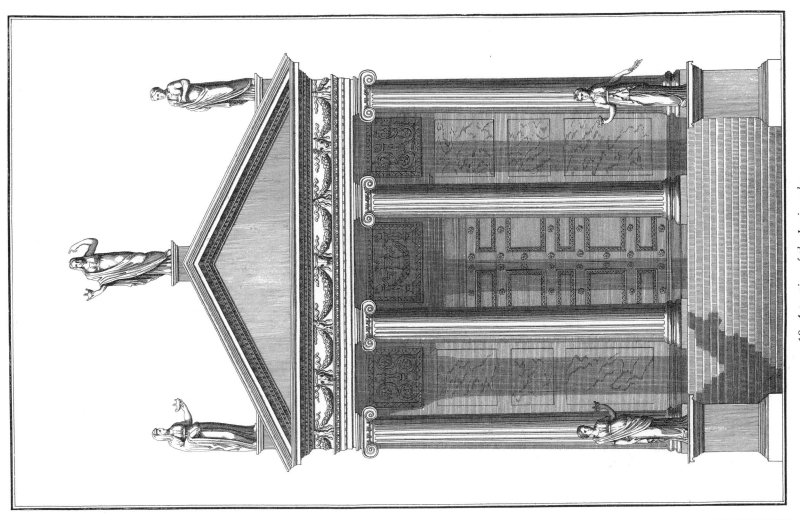

18. *A portico of the Ionic order.*

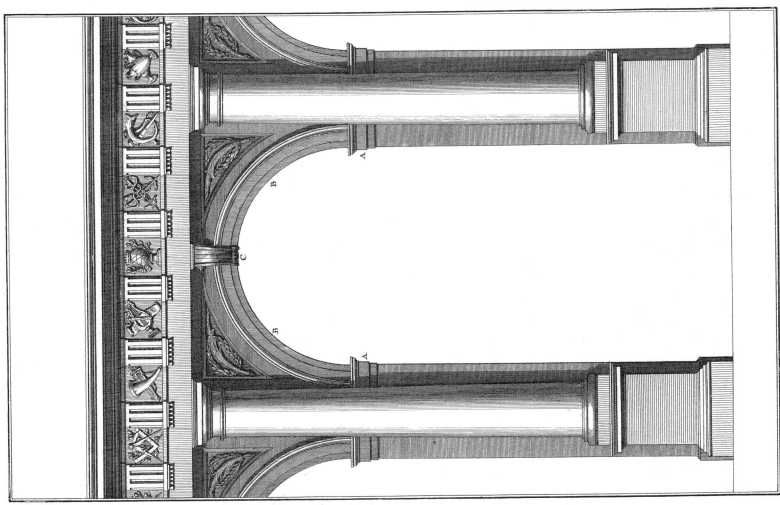

17. *A portico of the Doric order.*

9

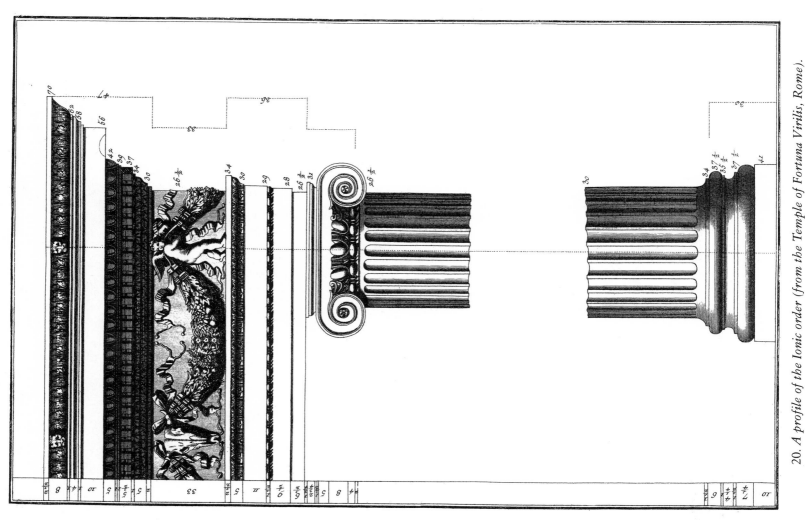

20. *A profile of the Ionic order (from the Temple of Fortuna Virilis, Rome).*

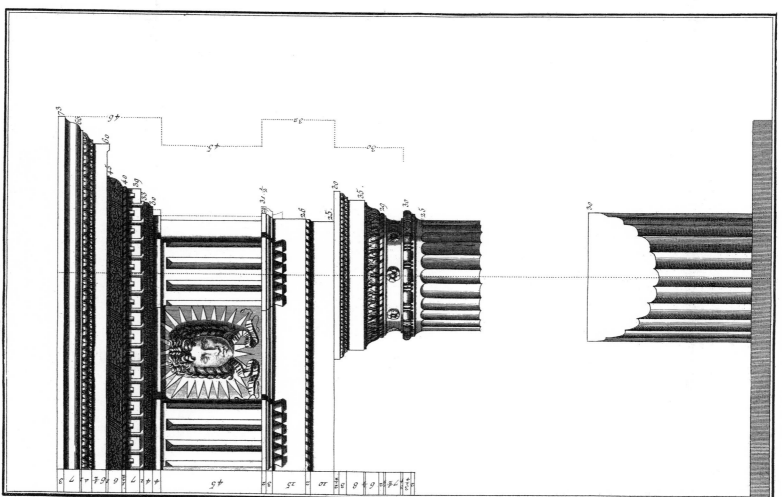

19. *A profile of the Doric order (from the Baths of Diocletian, Rome).*

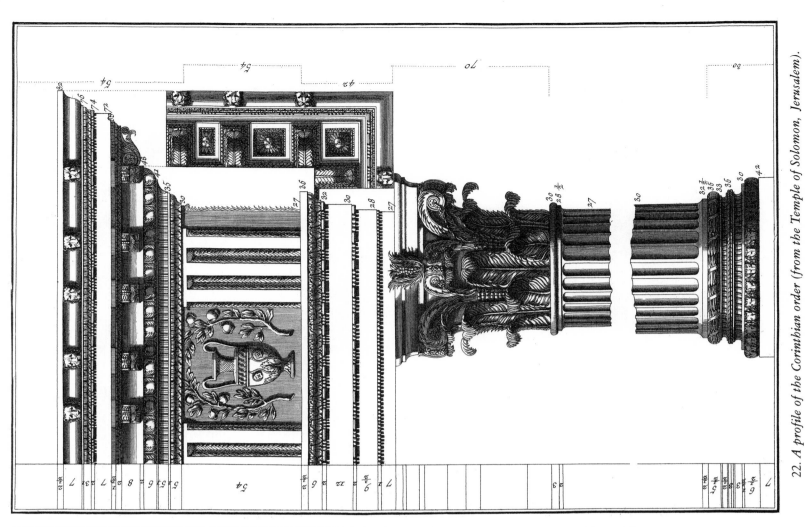

22. *A profile of the Corinthian order (from the Temple of Solomon, Jerusalem).*

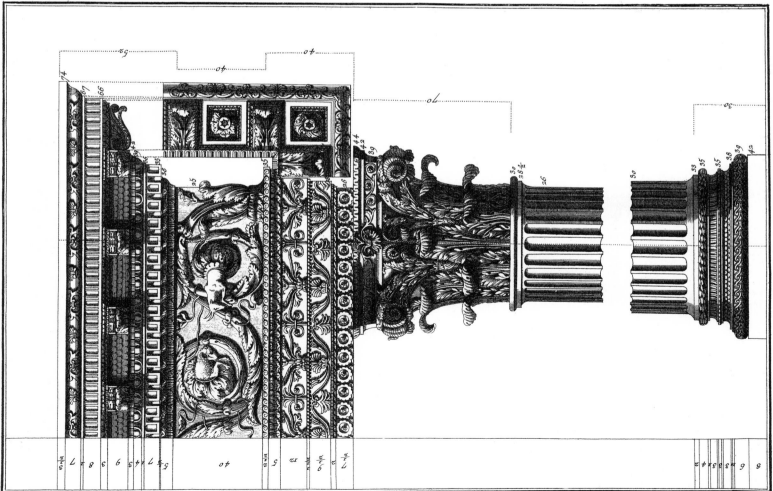

21. *A profile of the Corinthian order (from the Baths of Diocletian, Rome).*

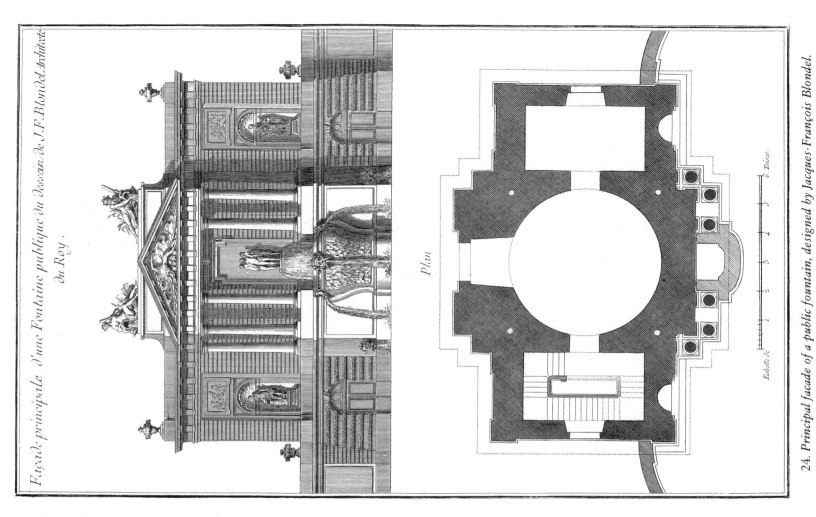

Façade principale d'une Fontaine publique du Dessein de J.F.Blondel Architecte du Roy.

Plan

Echelle &c.

6. Toises.

24. Principal facade of a public fountain, designed by Jacques-François Blondel.

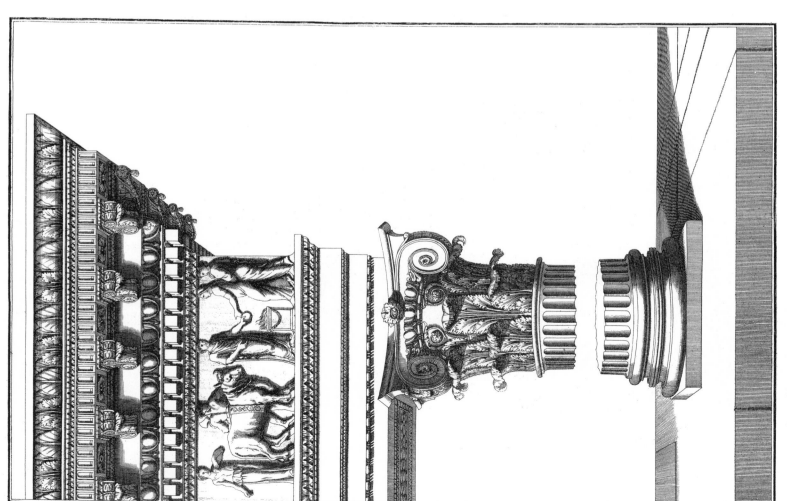

23. A profile of the Composite order (from the Arch of Titus, Rome).

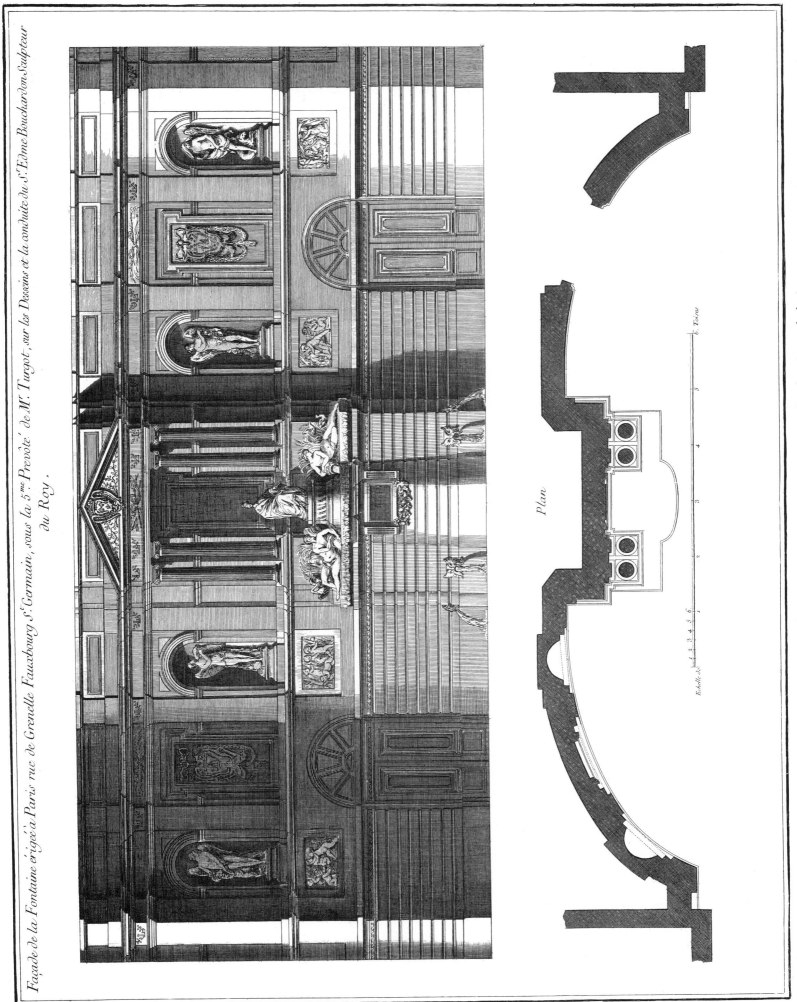

Façade de la Fontaine érigée à Paris rue de Grenelle Fauxbourg St.Germain, sous la 5.me Prevoté de Mr. Turgot, sur les Dessins et la conduite du S.t Edme Bouchardon Sculpteur du Roy.

Plan

Echelle de 1 2 3 4 5 6   6. Toises

25. Facade of Grenelle Fountain, Faubourg St.-Germain, Paris (elevation and plan).

13

Colonnade du Louvre.

Echelle de _____ 5 ____ 10 ____ 15 ____ 20 ____ 25 ____ 30 ____ 35 ____ 40. Toises

26. Colonnade of the Louvre, Paris (elevation and plan).

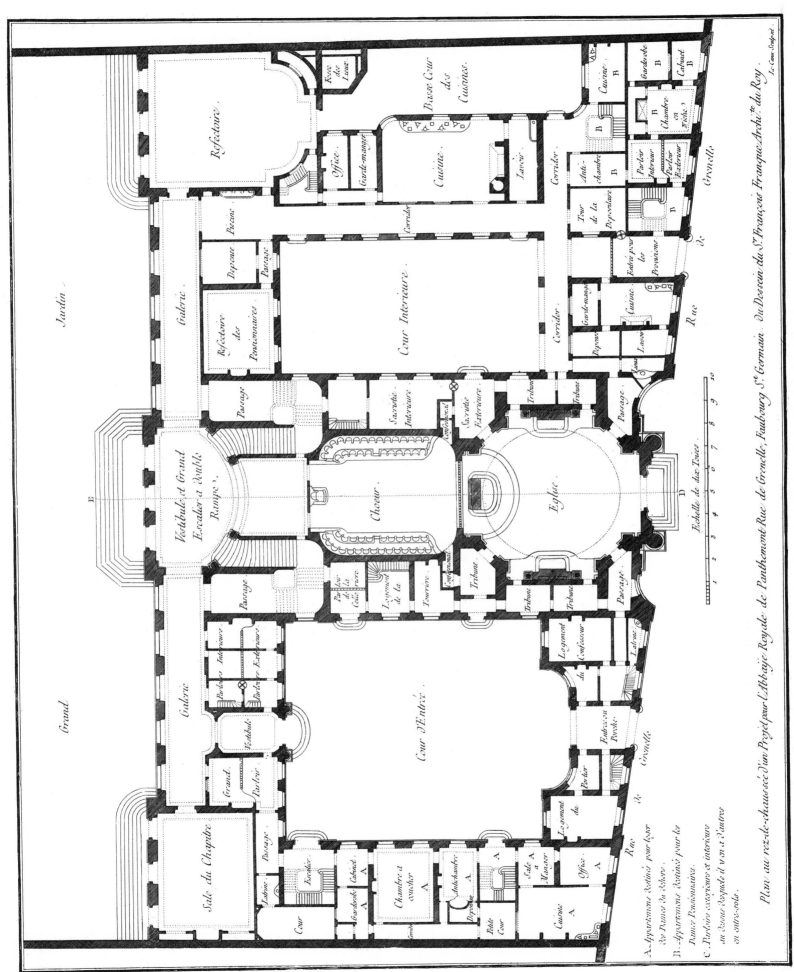

27. Ground-floor plan, Abbey of Panthemont, Paris. [Projected building.]

Plan du premier Étage du projet de l'Église et de l'Abbaye de Panthemont.

Jardin

Bucher

Latrines

Dortoir

Chambre de la Maîtresse des Novices

Chambre

Chambres

des

Novices

Chambre

Cour

Cour intérieure

Corridor

Corridor

Cuisine

Garderobe

Cabinet

Chambre en niche

Parloir

Parloir intérieur

Rue de Grenelle

Chambre

Garde robe

Antichambre

Chambre

Cabinet

Parloir

Parloir extérieur

Anti Chambre

Terrasse

Tribune

Tribune

Tribune

Tribune

Tribune

Tribune

Choeur

Église

Terrasse

Tribune

Tribune

Tribune

Tribune

Chambre

Cabinet

Chambre

Garderobe

Corridor

Garderobe

Corridor

Chambre

Rue de Grenelle

Échelle de 1 2 3 4 5 6 7 8 9 10 Toises.

Réfectoire

Dortoir

Chauffoir

Dortoir

Religieuses

Chambres

des

Cuisine

Office

Cabinet

Garderobe

Salle à manger

Cabinet

Parloir domestique

Chambre en niche

Parloir intérieur

Parloir extérieur

Bibliothèque

garde robe

Cour

Garderobe

Cabinet

Chambre et cuisine

Garde robe

Corridor

Cour

Cour d'entrée

Cour

Garderobe

Chambre en Niche

Anti Chambre

Cabinet

Fr.çois Franque Architecte du Roy.

Le Canu Sculpsit.

28. Second-floor plan, Abbey of Panthemont.

16

Plan du second Etage de l'Abbaye de Panthemont.

Chambres ·

Dortoir

Grande Chambre Pour les Novices.

Eglise

Cour.

Cour.

Cour.

Cour.

Cour.

Cour.

Cour.

Chambre

Chambre

Chambre des Sœurs Converses.

Piece a Repasser le Linge.

Lingerie

Antichambre

Corridor.

Cuisine.

Escalier

Chambre

Garderobe.

Cabinet.

Chambre

Antichambre

Chambre

Antichambre

Chambre

Depot

Gard.e Meuble.

Gard.e robe

Chambre

Chambre

Cabinet

Garderobe

Domestique.

Chambre de

Garderobe.

Garderobe.

Corridor.

Chambre

Chambre

10 Toises.

Fr.me François Arch.te du Roy.

Le Canu Sculp.t

29. Third-floor plan, Abbey of Panthemont.

17

Elevation du Projet de la façade extérieure de l'Eglise et des Bâtiments de l'Abbaye Royale de Panthemont du côté de la rue de Grenelle.

30. Street facades of the Church and buildings, Abbey of Panthemont.

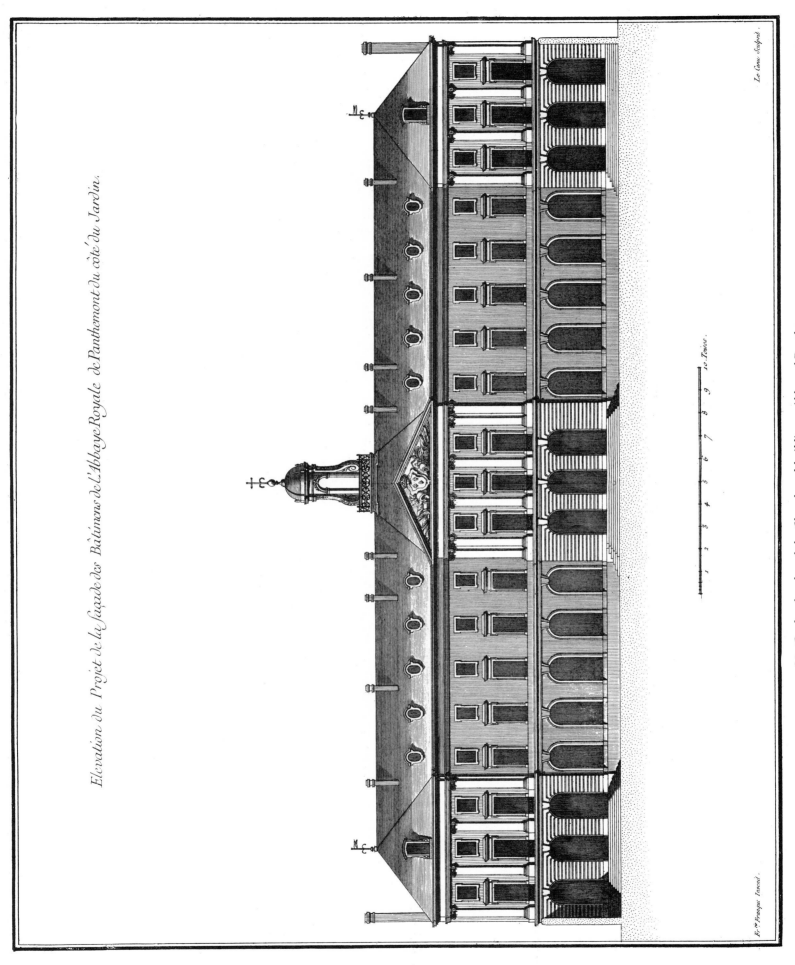

Elevation du Projet de la façade des Bâtimens de l'Abbaye Royale de Panthemont du côté du Jardin.

Fr.çois Franque Invenit.

Le Canu Sculpsit.

31. Garden facades of the Church and buildings, Abbey of Panthemont.

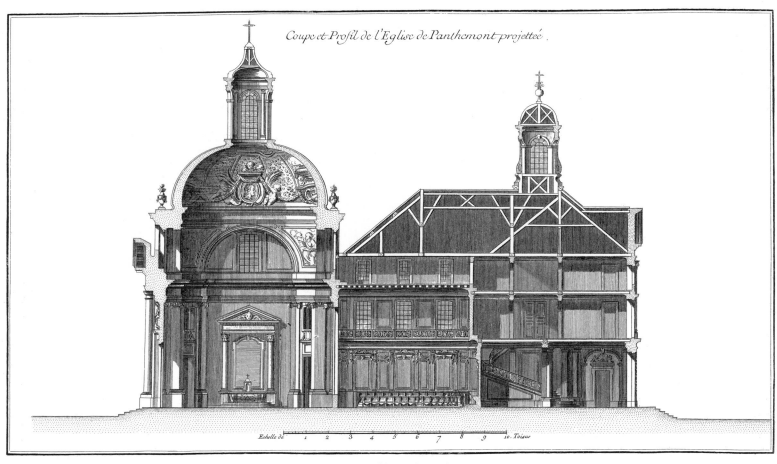

Coupe et Profil de l'Eglise de Panthemont projettée.

Echelle de 1 2 3 4 5 6 7 8 9 10. Toises

32. Section, Abbey of Panthemont.

Profil du Corps de Logis ou sont les Salles.

33. Section of main prison building, Brest, France.

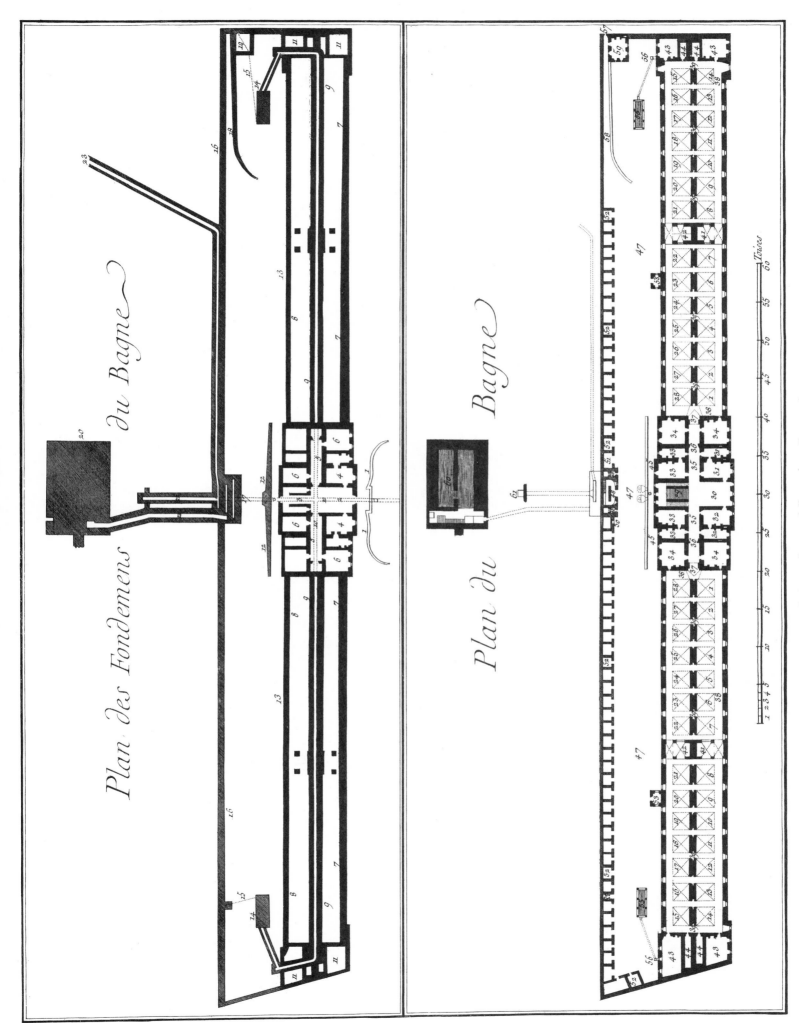

Plan des Fondemens

du Bagne

Plan du Bagne

34. Foundation and ground-floor plans, Brest prison.

21

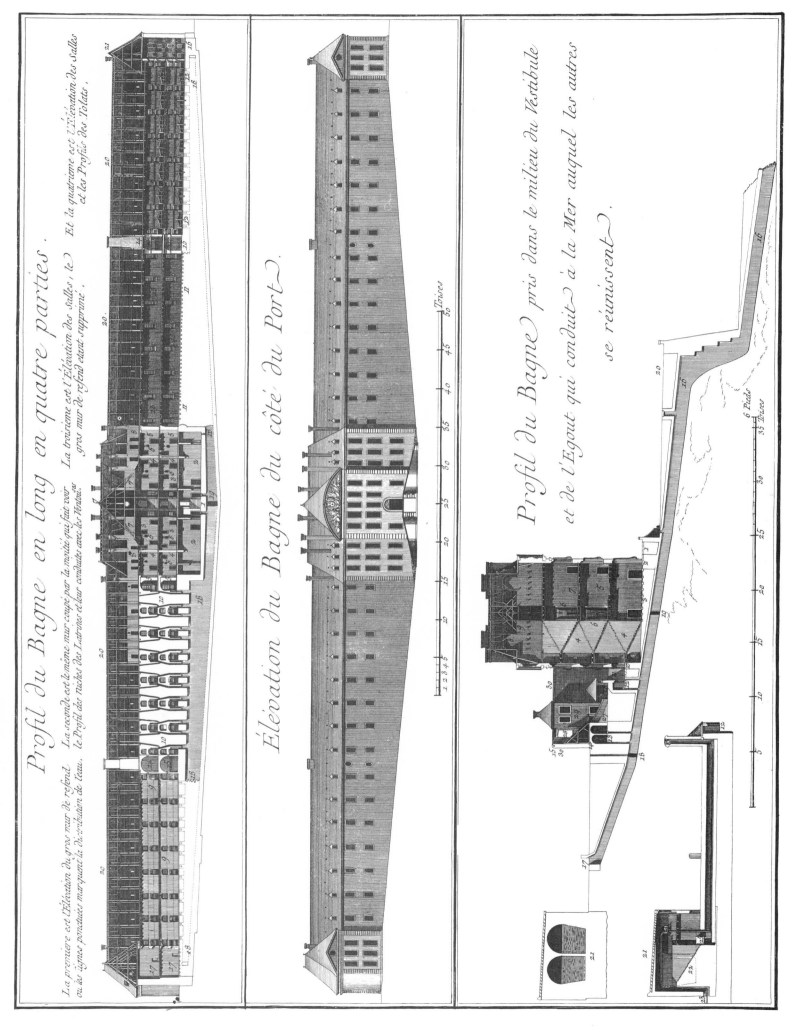

Profil du Bagne en long en quatre parties.

La première est l'élévation du gros mur de refent La seconde est le même mur coupé par la mulié qui fait voir Et la quatrième est l'élévation des Sudles, le
où les lignes ponctuées marquent la distribution de l'eau. le Profil des niches des Latrines et leur conduits avec les Vestuli. gros mur de refend étant supprimé.
La troisième est l'élévation des Sudles, le et les Profils des Soldats.

Élévation du Bagne du côté du Port.

Profil du Bagne pris dans le milieu du Vestibule
et de l'Egout qui conduit à la Mer auquel les autres
se réunissent.

35. Sections and an elevation, Brest prison.

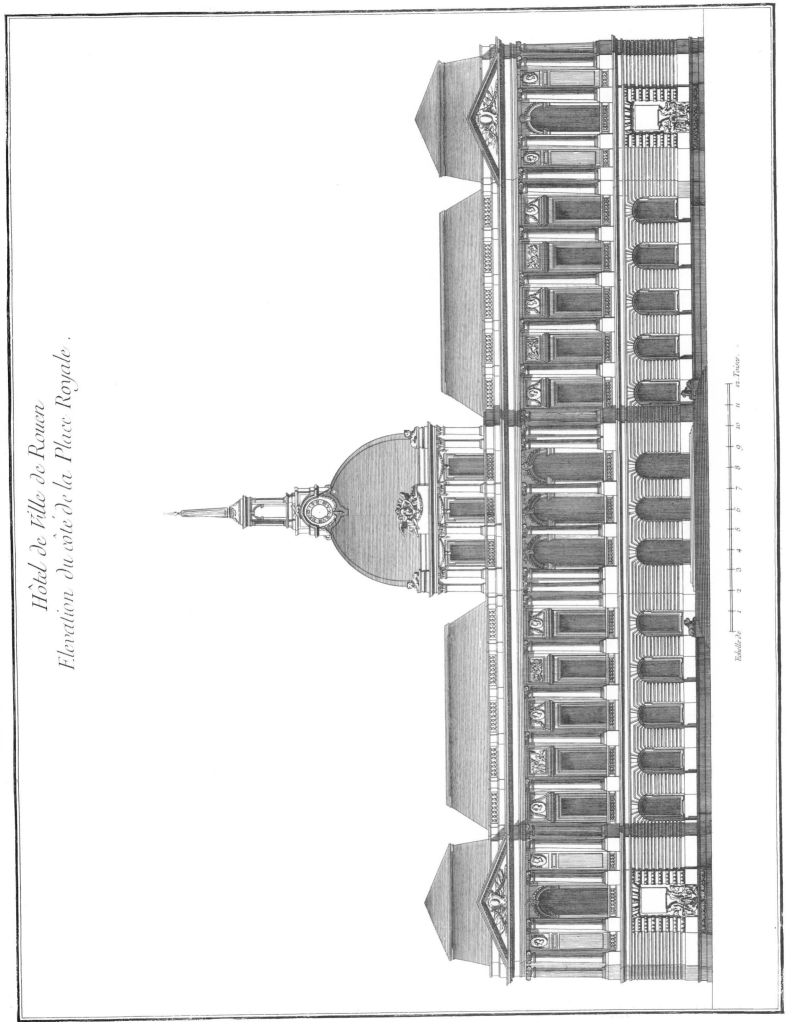

Hôtel de Ville de Rouen
Elevation du côté de la Place Royale .

Echelle de 1 2 3 4 5 6 7 8 9 10 11 12 Toises .

36. Principal elevation of the Town Hall, Rouen, France.

23

Plan au Rez de Chaussée d'un grand Hôtel du dessein de Jacques françois Blondel Architecte du Roy.

37. Ground-floor plan of a mansion, designed by Jacques-François Blondel.

Elevation du côté de l'entrée d'un grand Hôtel avec ses dépendances,
du Dessein de Jacques François Blondel Architecte du Roy.

38. Facades of a mansion and its outbuildings, designed by Jacques-François Blondel.

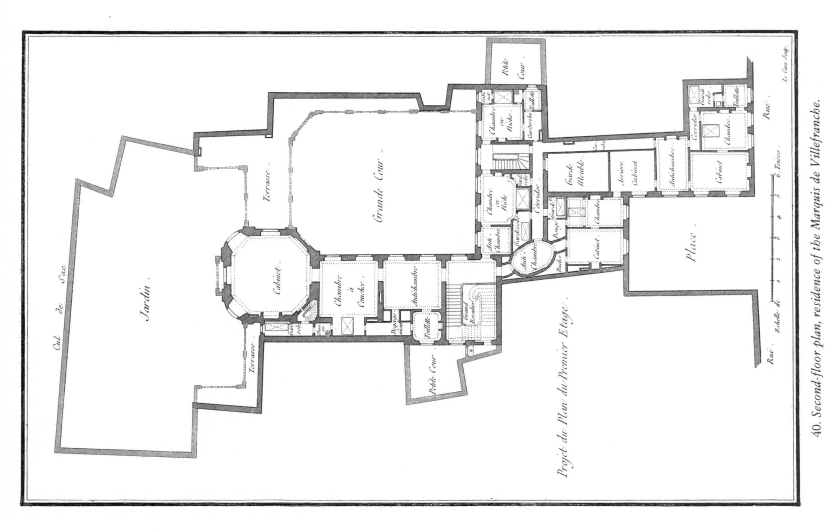

40. Second-floor plan, residence of the Marquis de Villefranche.

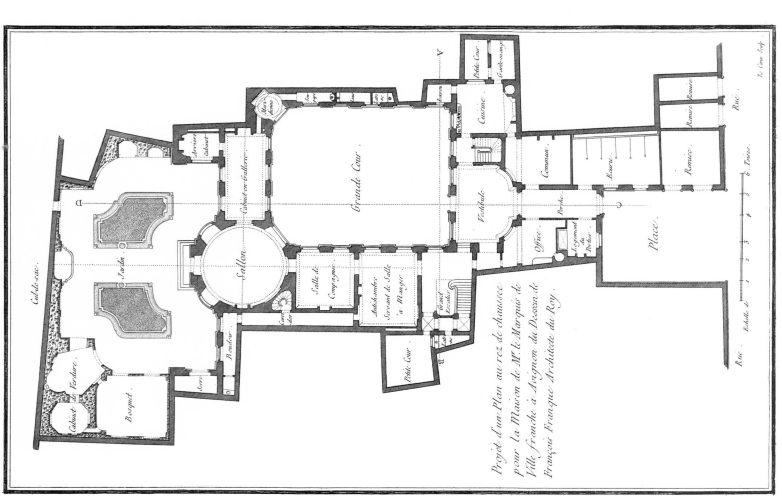

39. Ground-floor plan of the residence of the Marquis de Villefranche, Avignon, France, designed by François Franque.

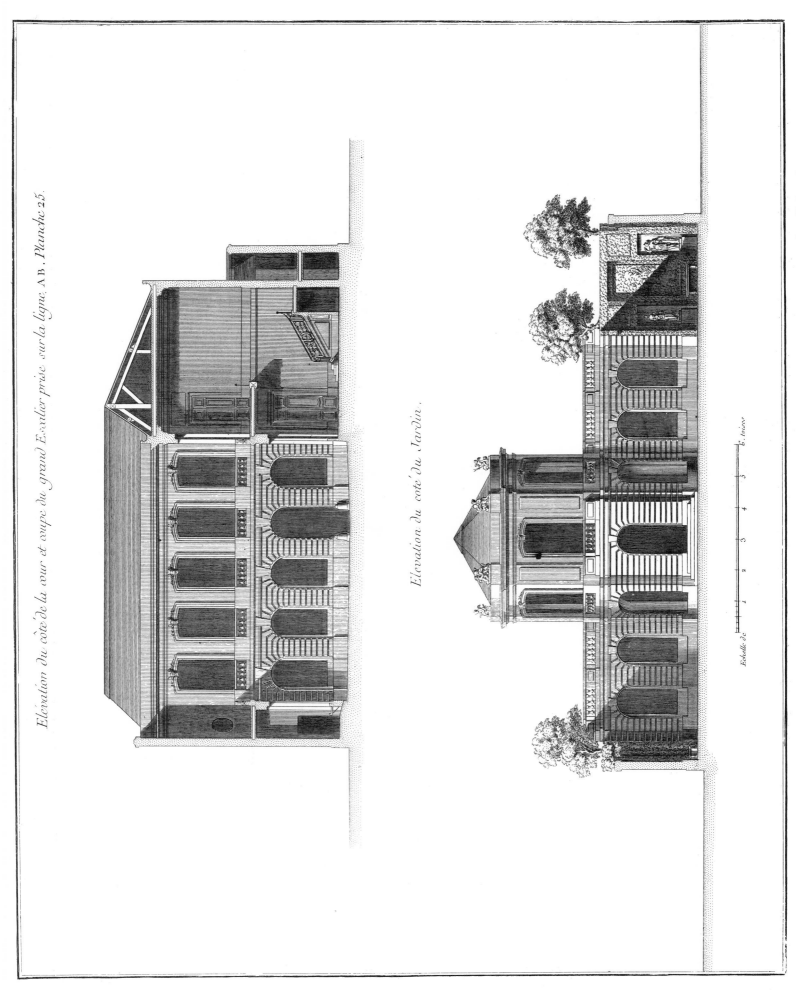

Elévation du côté de la cour et coupe du grand Escalier prise sur la ligne, A B. Planche 25.

Elévation du côté du Jardin.

Echelle de ... 1 ... 2 ... 3 ... 4 ... 5 ... 6. toises

41. *Transverse section (corresponds to line A–B, plate 39, above) and garden façade, residence of the Marquis de Villefranche.*

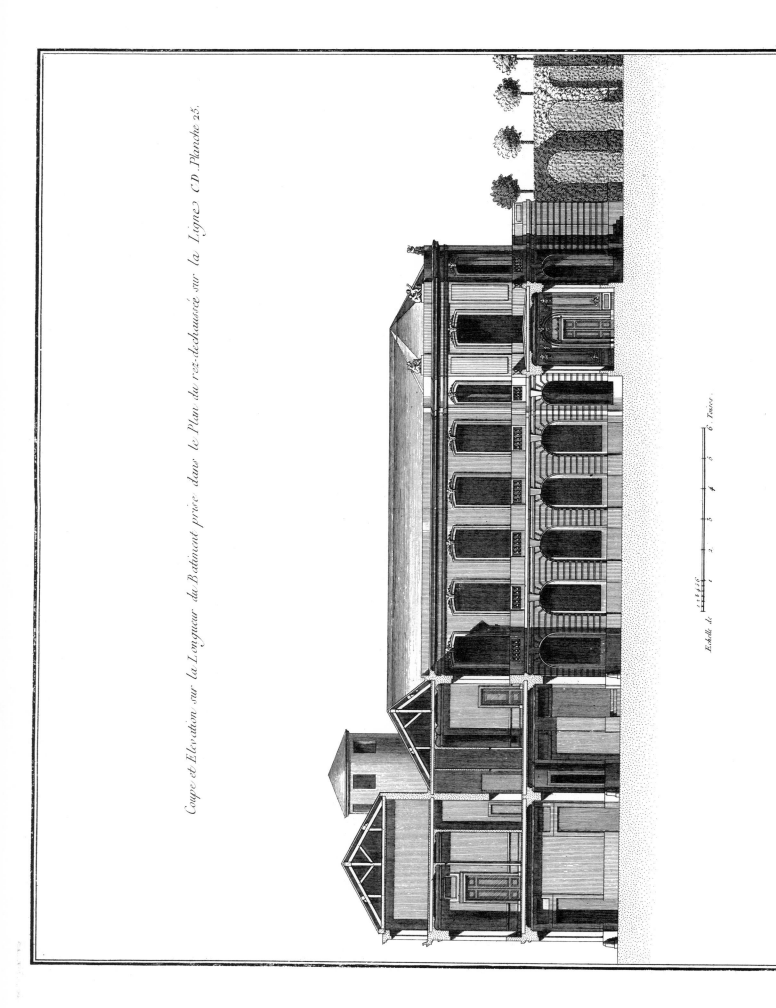

Coupe et Elevation sur la Longueur du Batiment prise dans le Plan du rez-dechaussée sur la Ligne CD. Planche 25.

Echelle de: 1 2 3 4 5 6 7 ... 1 2 3 4 5 6. Toises.

42. Longitudinal section (corresponds to line C–D, plate 39, above), residence of the Marquis de Villefranche.

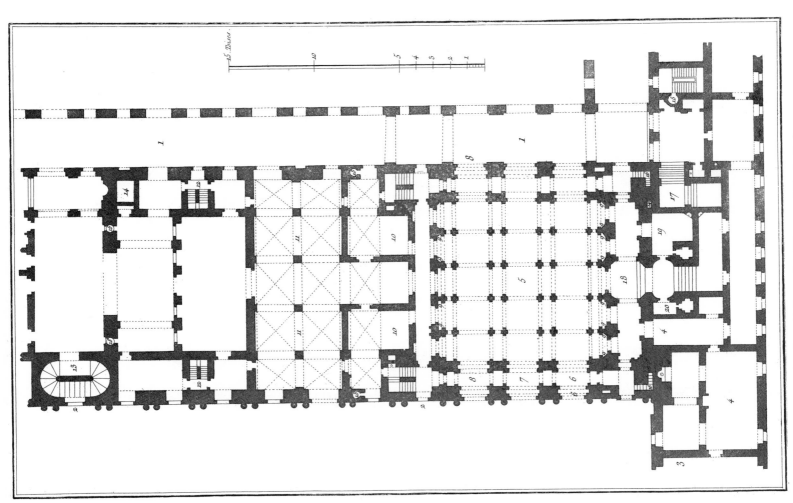

44. *Proportions of the auditorium, Theater of Turin.*

43. *Ground-floor plan, Theater of Turin, Italy.*

29

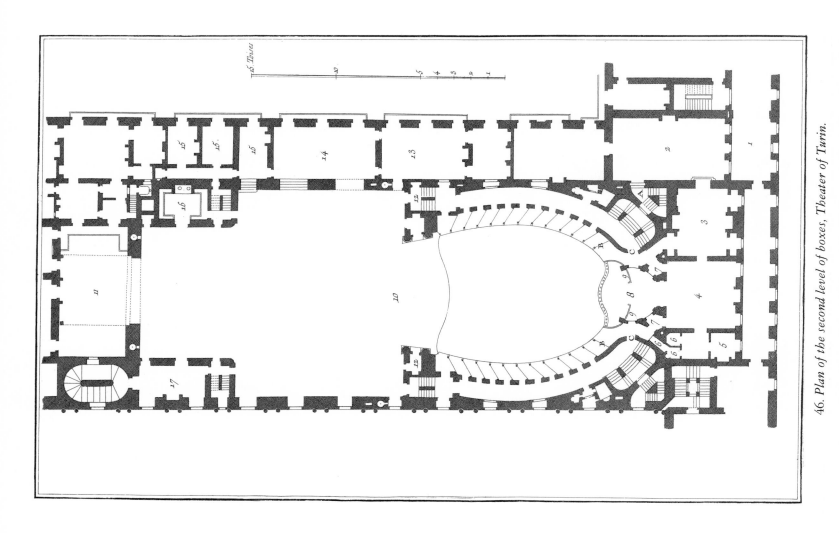

46. *Plan of the second level of boxes, Theater of Turin.*

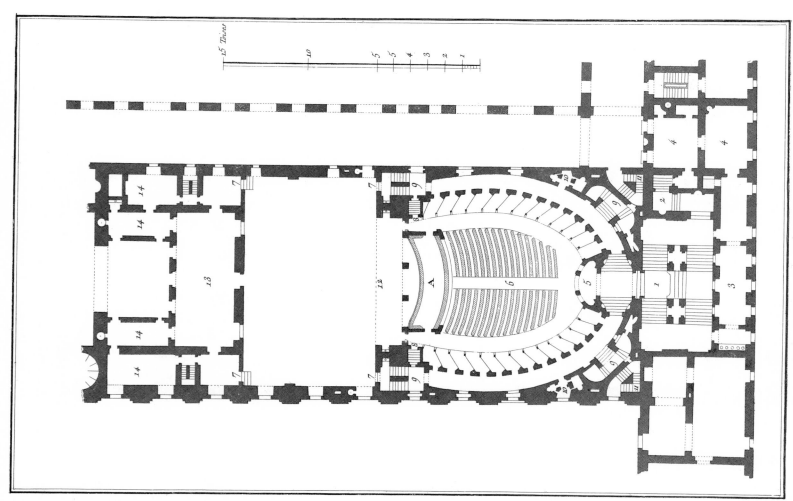

45. *Plan of the orchestra and first level of boxes, Theater of Turin.*

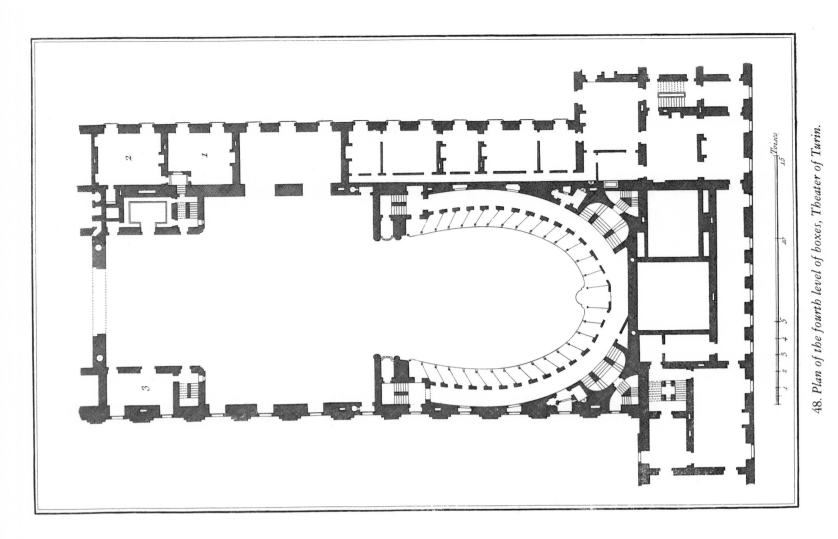

48. *Plan of the fourth level of boxes, Theater of Turin.*

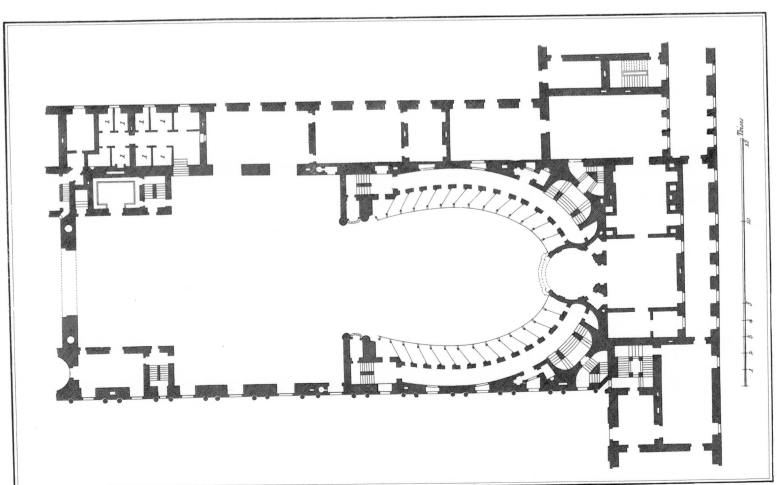

47. *Plan of the third level of boxes, Theater of Turin.*

31

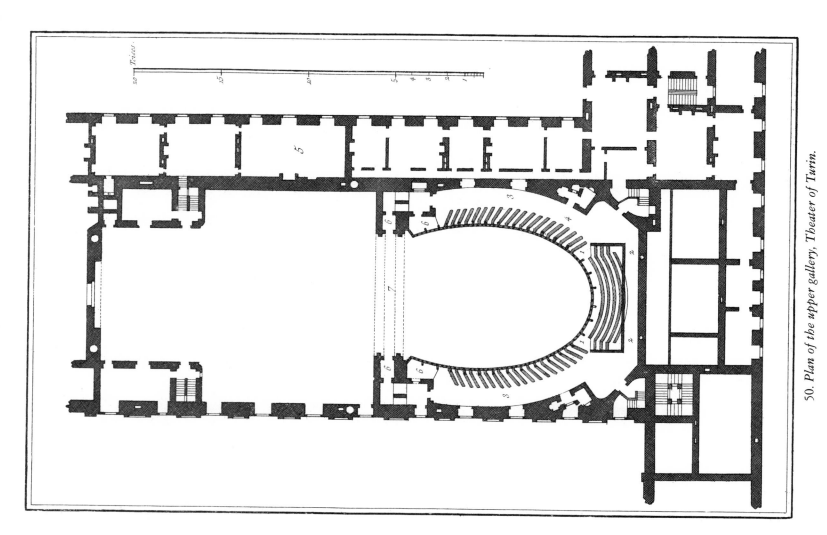

50. *Plan of the upper gallery, Theater of Turin.*

49. *Plan of the fifth level of boxes, Theater of Turin.*

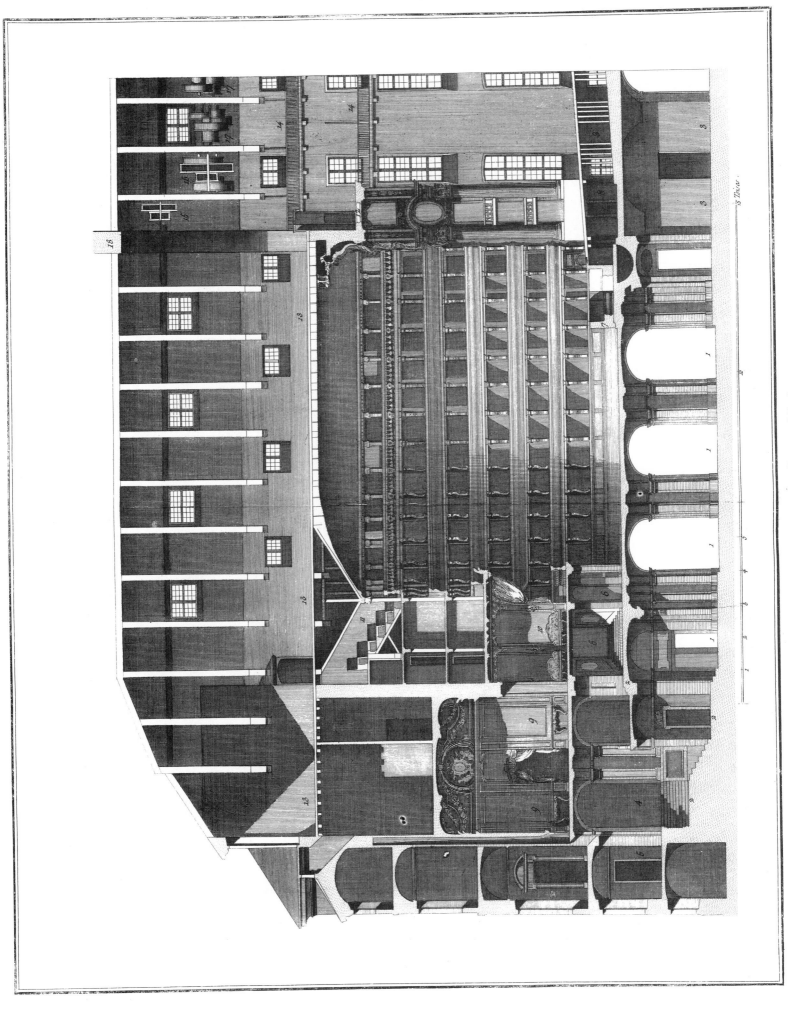

51. *Longitudinal section, Theater of Turin.*

33

52. *Transverse section, Theater of Turin.*

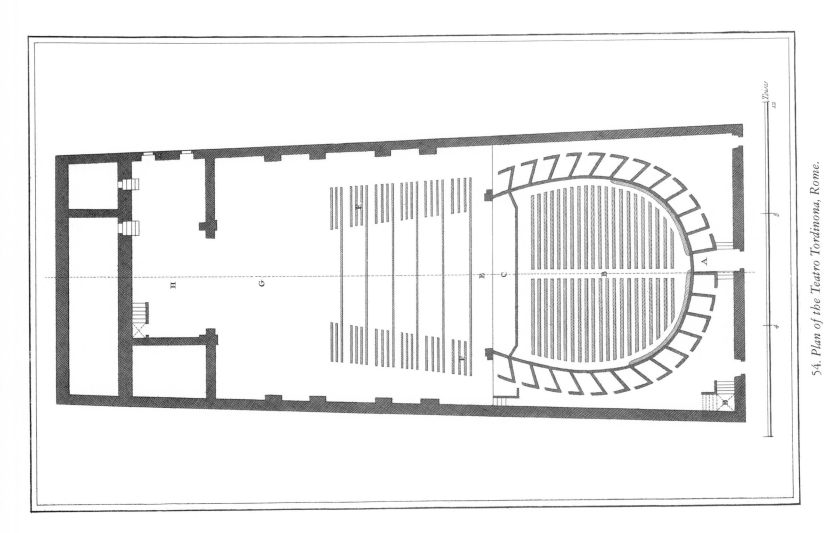

54. *Plan of the Teatro Tordinona, Rome.*

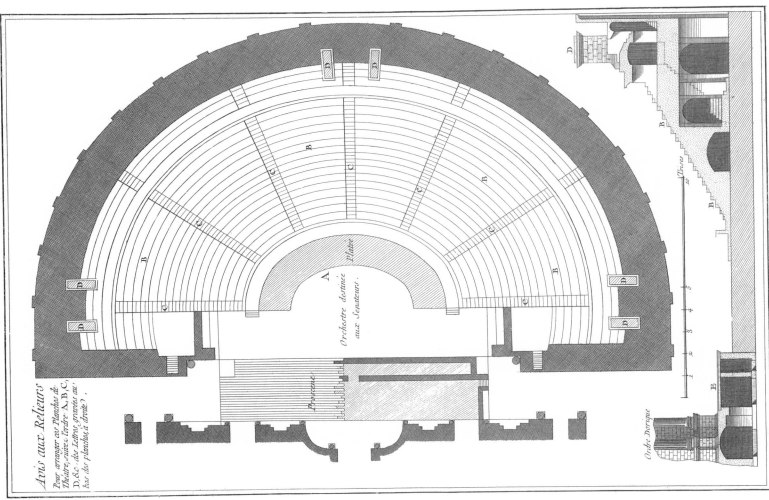

Orchestre destinée aux Senateurs.

53. *Plan of the Roman theater at Herculaneum.*

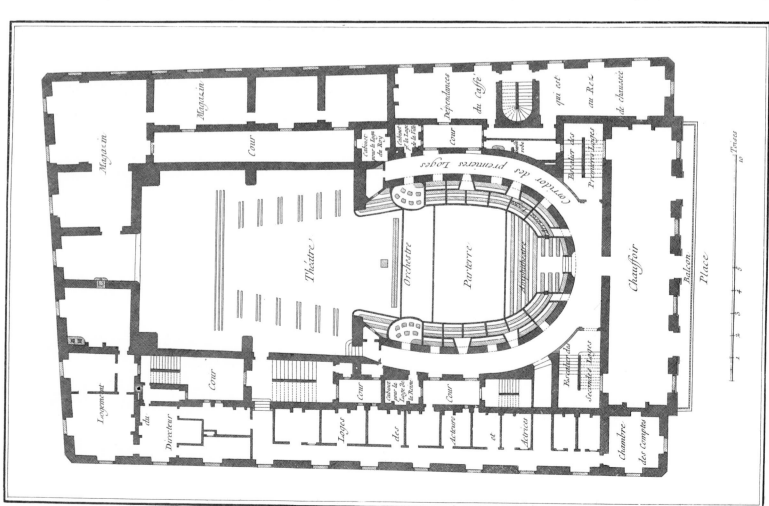

56. Sections and facade, Salle de Comédie, Lyon.

55. Plan of the Salle de Comédie, Lyon, France.

Magazin

Magazin

Cour

Théatre

Logement du Directeur

Cour

Loges

Cour

des

Acteurs

Cabinet pour la Loge de la Reine

Cour

et

Actrices

Chambre des Comptes

Cabinet pour la Loge du Roy

Cabinet de la Loge de la Fille

Dépendances

du Caffé

Cour

qui est

au Rez

de chaussée

Escalier des Premieres Loges

Corridor des premieres Loges

Orchestre

Parterre

Amphithéatre

Escalier des Secondes Loges

Chauffoir

Balcon

Place

36

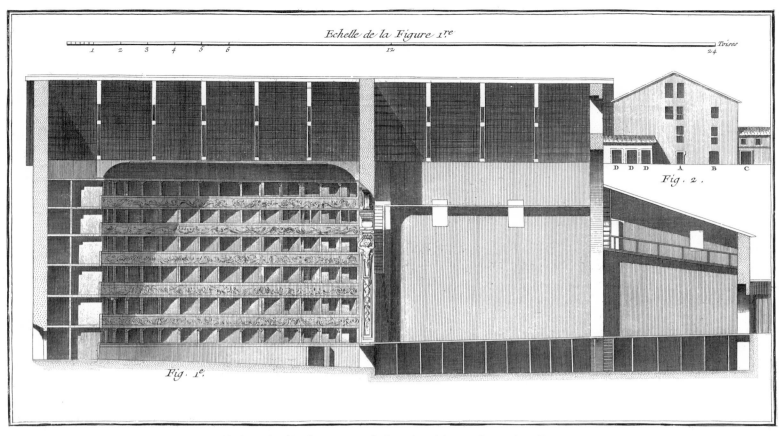

58. *Longitudinal section and elevation, Teatro Argentina, Rome.*

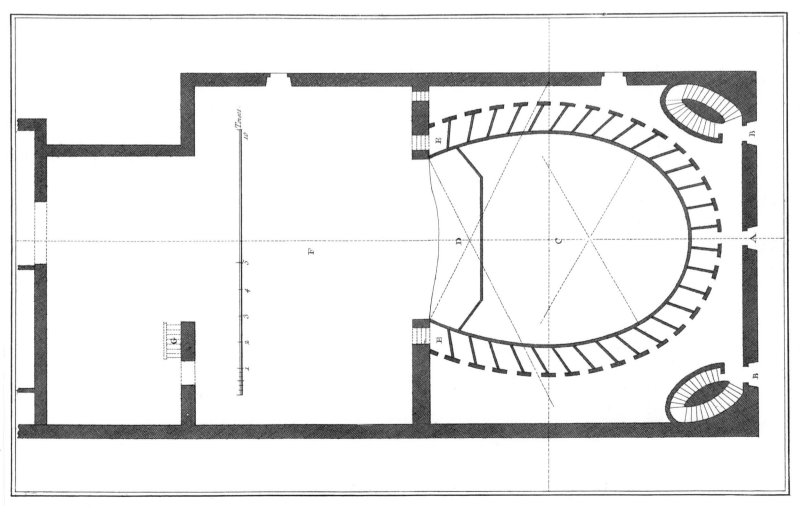

57. *Plan of the Teatro Argentina, Rome.*

59. *Plan of the Royal Theater of San Carlo, Naples, Italy.*

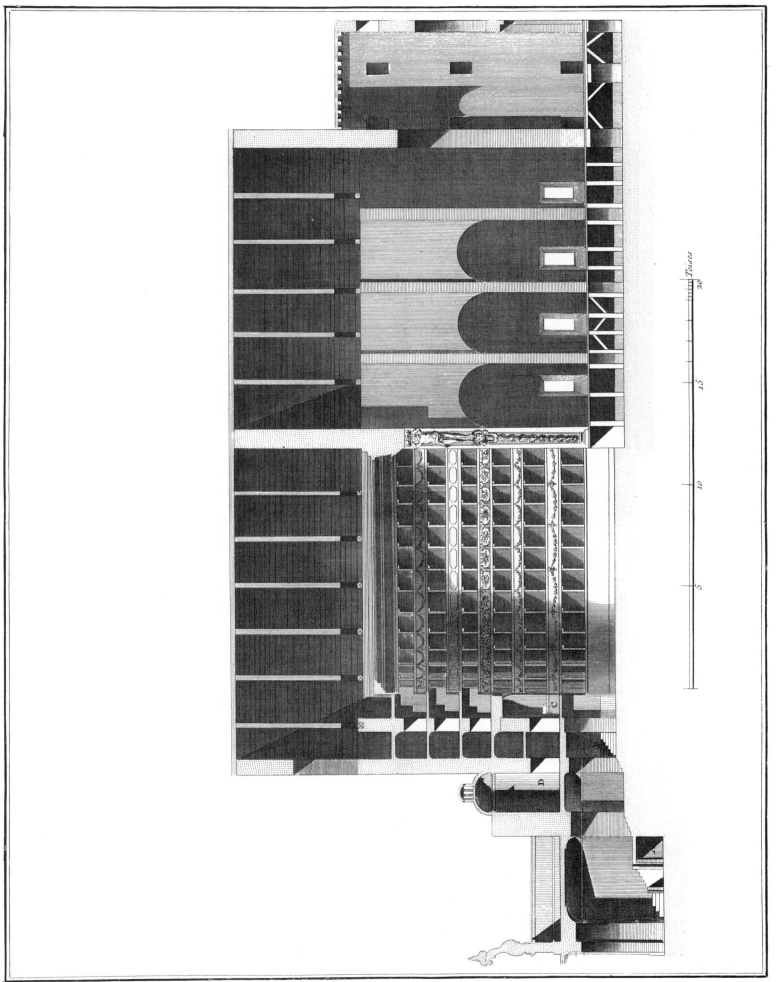

60. *Longitudinal section, Royal Theater of San Carlo, Naples.*

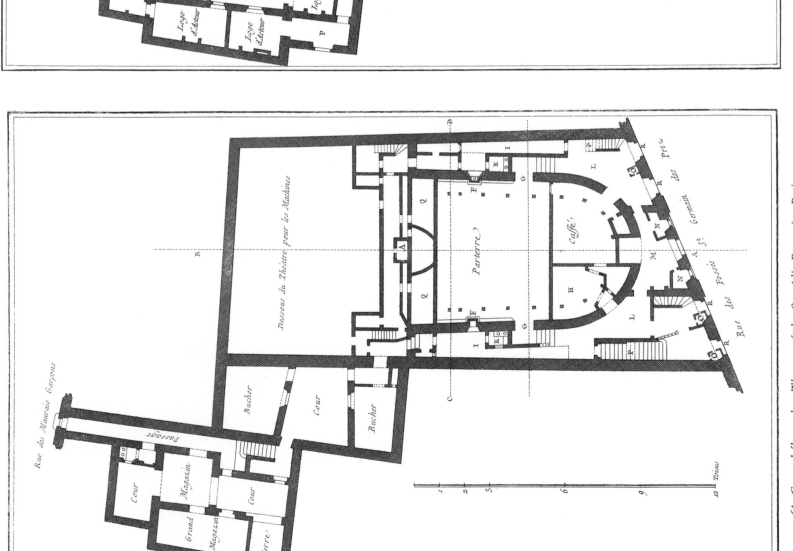

62. *Second-floor plan, Comédie-Française.*

61. *Ground-floor plan, Theater of the Comédie-Française, Paris.*

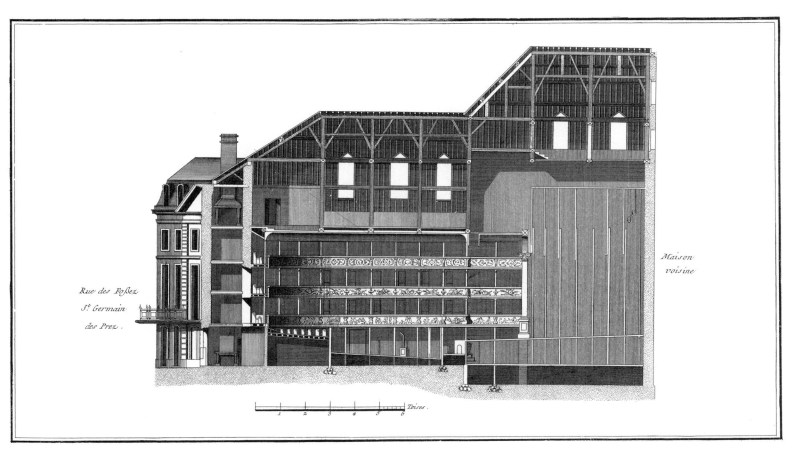

Rue des Foßez
St. Germain
des Prez.

Maison
voisine

Toises.
1   2   3   4   5   6

63. Longitudinal section, Comédie-Française.

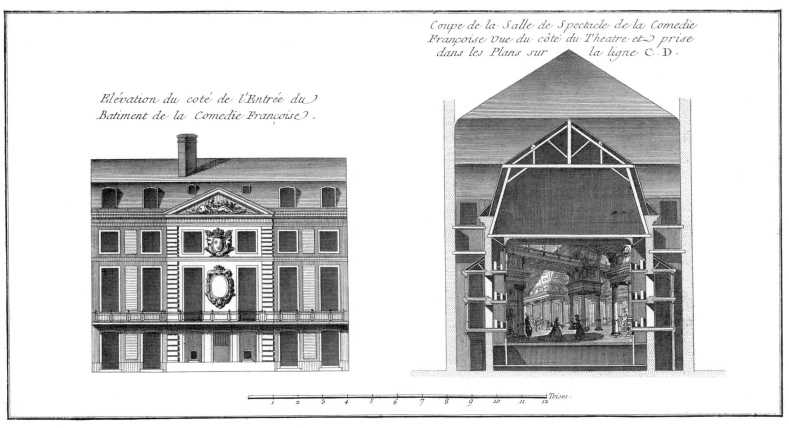

Elévation du coté de l'Entrée du
Batiment de la Comedie Francoise.

Coupe de la Salle de Spectacle de la Comedie
Françoise vue du côté du Theatre et prise
dans les Plans sur   la ligne C. D.

Toises.
1   2   3   4   5   6   7   8   9   10   11   12

64. Elevation and transverse section, Comédie-Française.

41

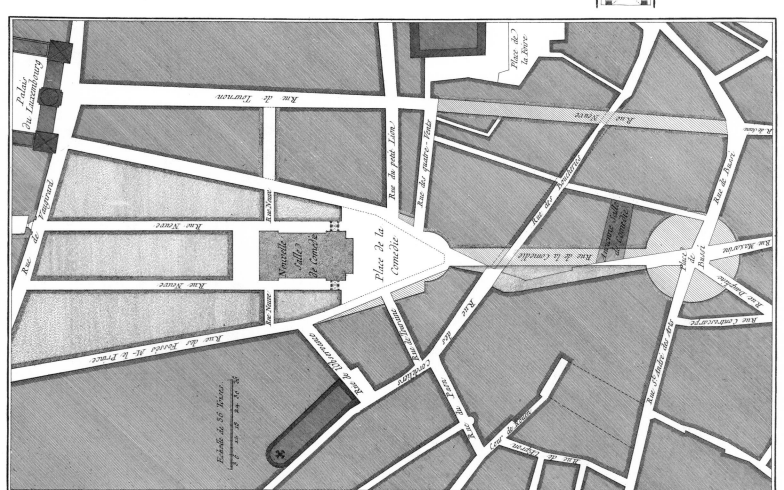

66. *Ground-floor plan, new Comédie-Française.*

Echelle de 1 2 3 4 5 6 7 8 9 10 Toises

65. *Location of the new theater of the Comédie-Française, Paris [since 1796, the Odéon].*

Echelle de 36 Toises 3 6 10 15 24 30 36

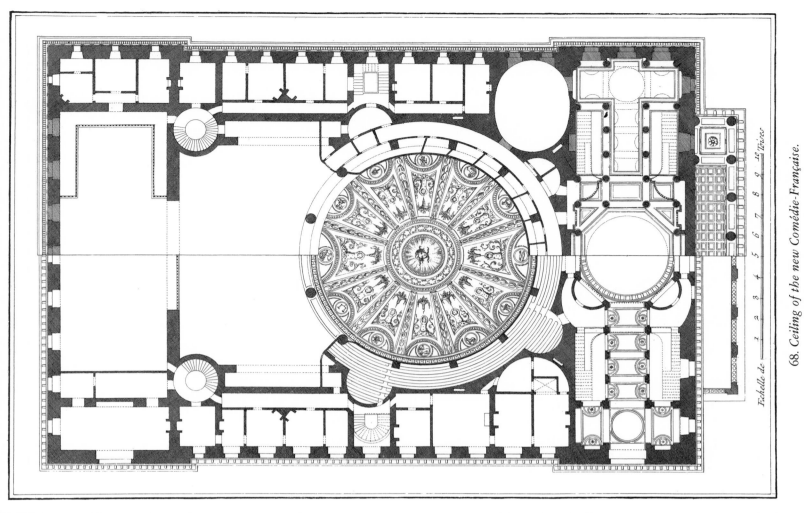

68. *Ceiling of the new Comédie-Française.*

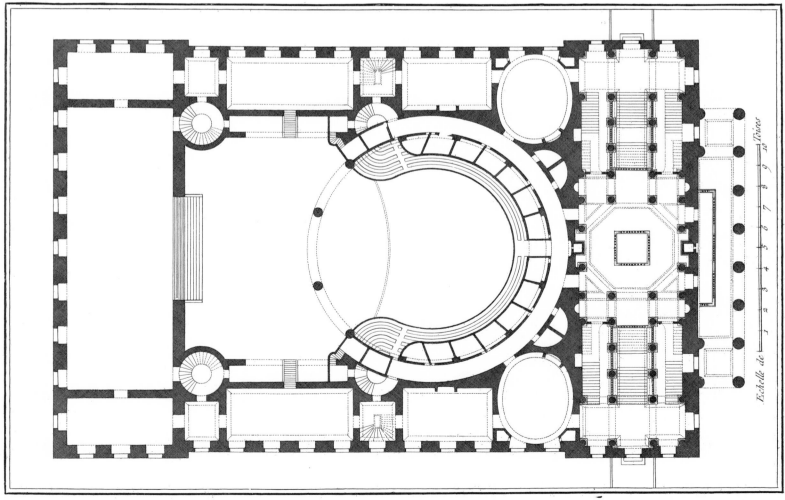

67. *Plan of the first level of boxes, new Comédie-Française.*

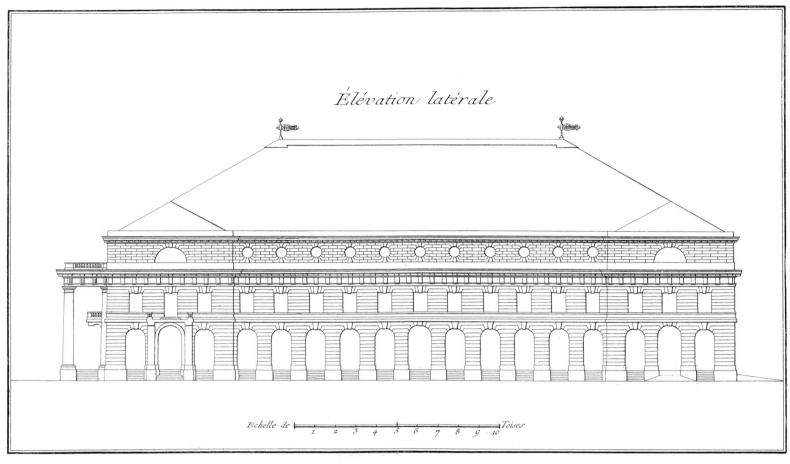

Élévation latérale

Echelle de |———|———|———|———|———|———|———|———|———|———| Toises
1 2 3 4 5 6 7 8 9 10

69. *Lateral elevation, new Comédie-Française.*

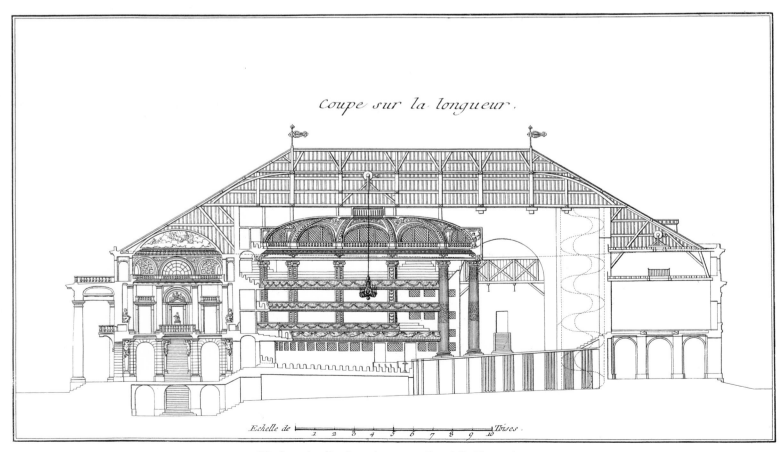

Coupe sur la longueur.

Echelle de |———|———|———|———|———|———|———|———|———|———| Toises
1 2 3 4 5 6 7 8 9 10

70. *Longitudinal section, new Comédie-Française.*

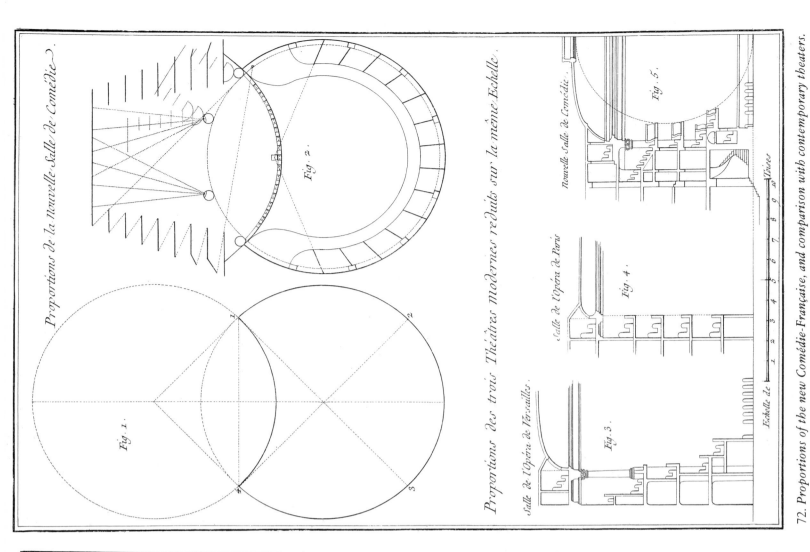

Proportions de la nouvelle Salle de Comédie.

Fig. 1.

Fig. 2.

Proportions des trois Théâtres modernes réduits sur la même Échelle.

Salle de l'Opéra de Versailles.

Fig. 3.

Salle de l'Opéra de Paris.

Fig. 4.

nouvelle salle de Comédie.

Fig. 5.

Échelle de · · · Toises

72. Proportions of the new Comédie-Française, and comparison with contemporary theaters.

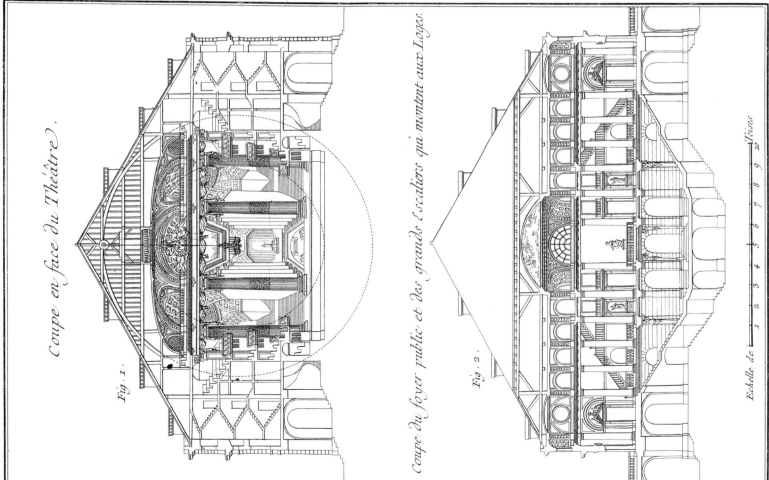

Coupe en face du Théâtre.

Fig. 1.

Coupe du foyer public et des grands Escaliers qui montent aux Loges.

Fig. 2.

Échelle de · · · Toises

71. Transverse sections, new Comédie-Française.

45

73. Façade, new Comédie-Française.

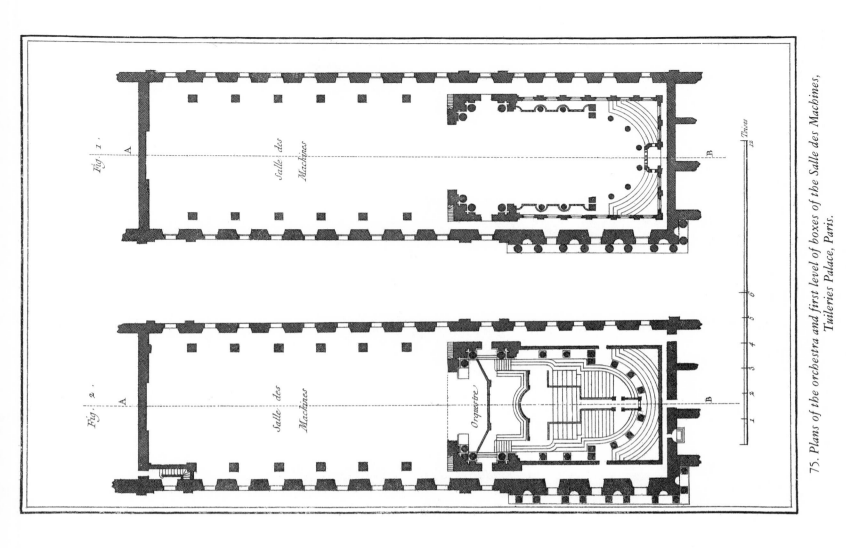

75. *Plans of the orchestra and first level of boxes of the Salle des Machines, Tuileries Palace, Paris.*

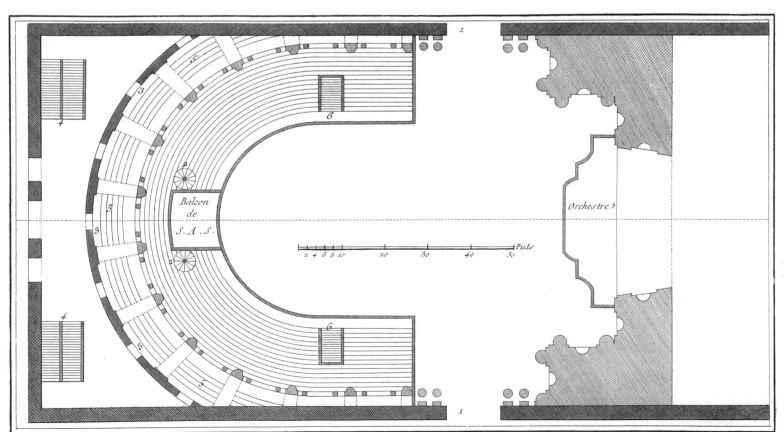

74. *Plan of the Theater of Parma, Italy.*

47

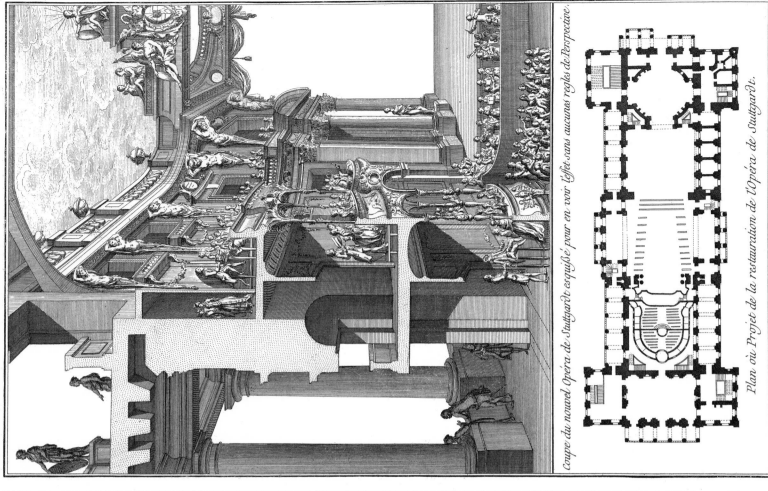

Coupe du nouvel Opéra de Stuttgardt esquissé pour en voir l'effet sans aucuns regles de Perspective.

Plan où Projet de la restauration de l'Opéra de Stuttgardt.

77. Transverse section and plan of the restored Opera House, Stuttgart, Germany.

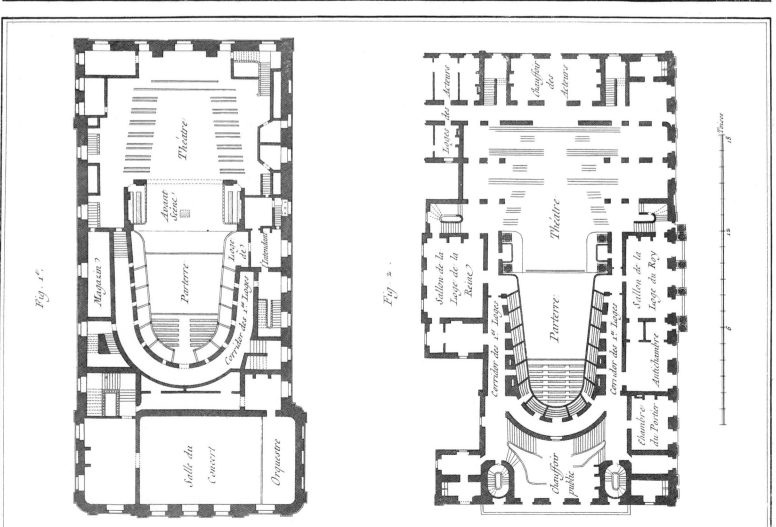

Fig. 1.

Magazin

Theatre

Avant Scene

Parterre

Loge d.°

Corridor des 1.es Loges

Intendant

Salle du Concert

Orquestre

Fig. 2.

Loges des Acteurs

Chauffoir des Acteurs

Sallon de la Loge de la Reine

Theatre

Corridor des 1.es Loges

Parterre

Corridor des 1.es Loges

Sallon de la Loge du Roy

Chambre du Portier

Antichambre

Chauffoir public

6   12   18   Toises

76. Plans of the Playhouse of Montpellier and the Theater of Metz, France.

Maisons Particulieres

Publique

Cour

Cour des Bons

Enfans

Rue)

Saint

Honoré

Cour

Cour

Echelle de 30 Toises.

125 0   12   18   24   30   36   42   48   54   60   90   120   150   180   Pieds.

78. Ground-floor plan, Paris Opera.

49

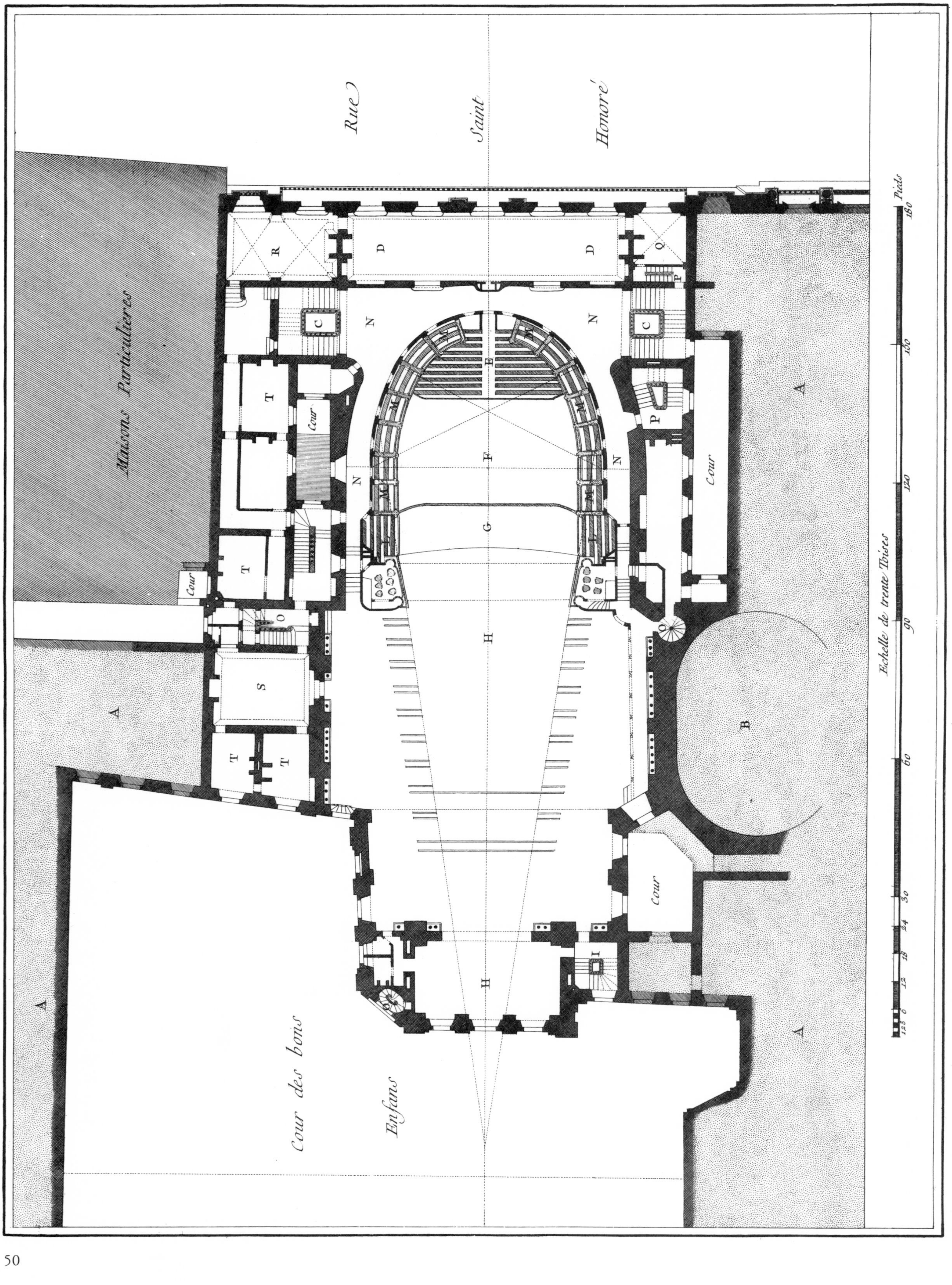

79. Plan of the auditorium, Paris Opera.

Rue Saint Honoré

Maisons Particulières

Cour des bons Enfans

Echelle de trente Toises

50

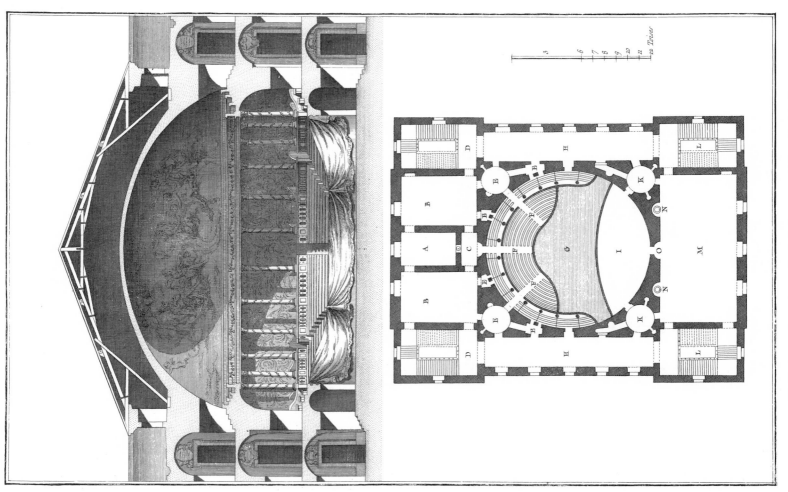

80. *Transverse section and plan of a proposed concert hall.*

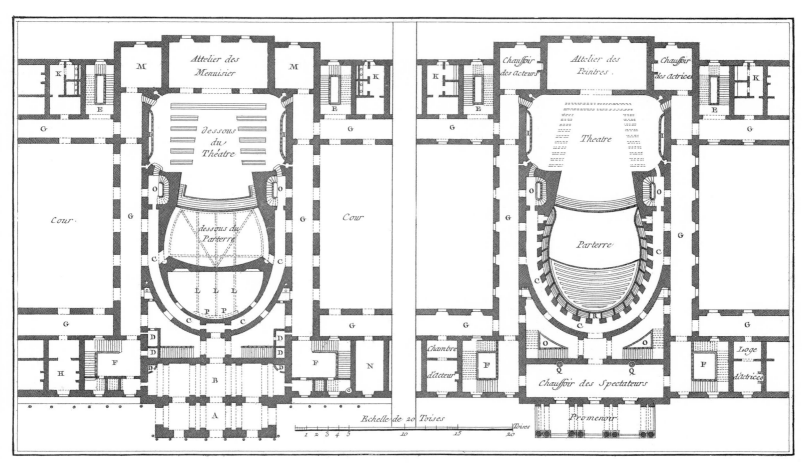

81. *Ground-floor and auditorium plans of a proposed theater.*

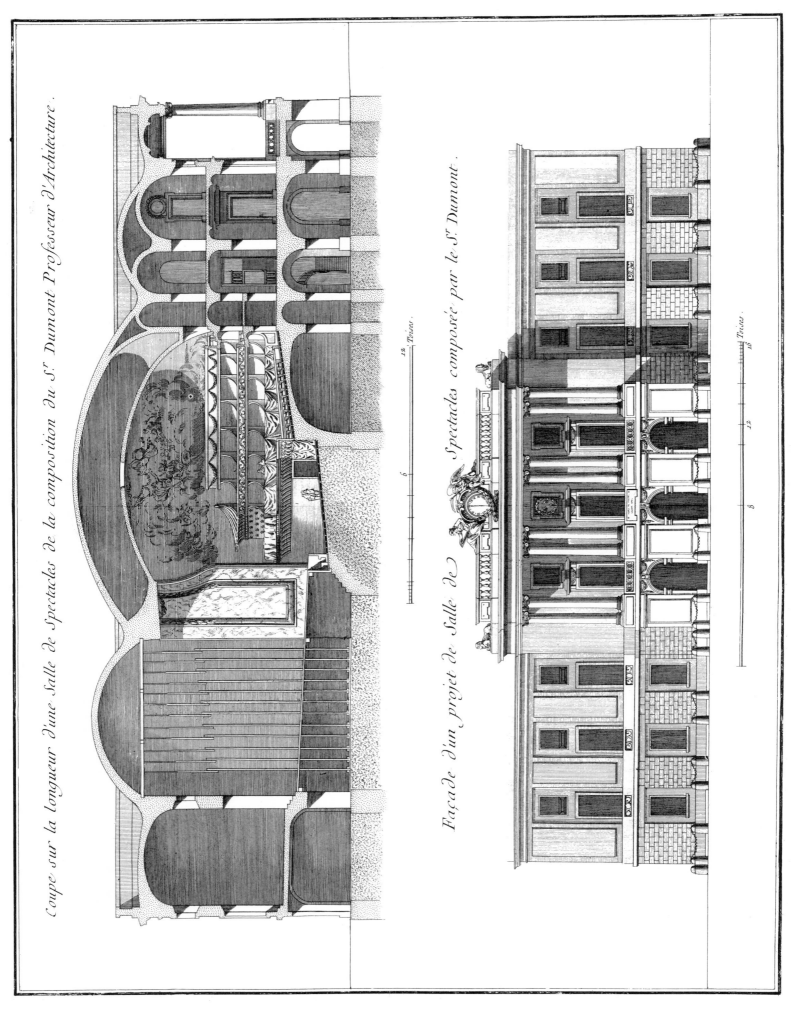

Coupe sur la longueur d'une Salle de Spectacles de la composition du S.ͬ Dumont Professeur d'Architecture.

Façade d'un projet de Salle de Spectacles composée par le S.ͬ Dumont.

82. Longitudinal section and facade of a proposed theater.

Echelle de 1 2 3 4 5 6   12 Pieds

83. *Transverse section of drawing-room in the new suite of the Royal Palace.*

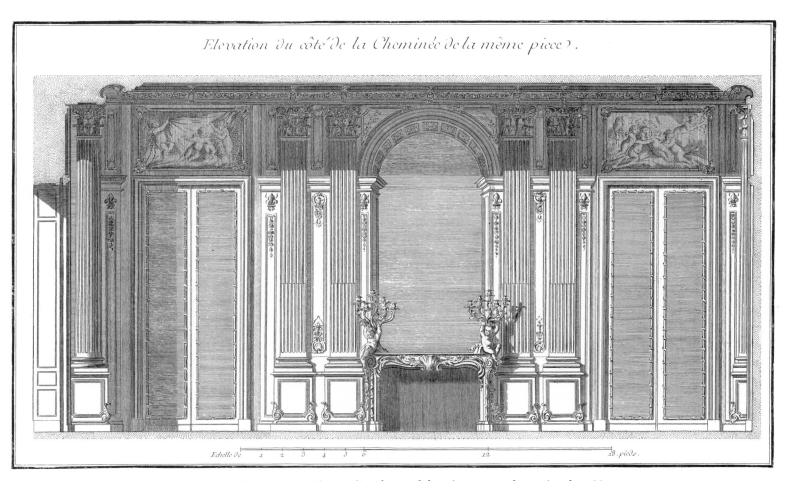

Echelle de 1 2 3 4 5 6   12   18 pieds.

84. *Longitudinal section (facing fireplace) of drawing-room shown in plate 83.*

Elevation de la Salle de Jeu du côté de la porte qui donne entrée au Sallon.

Echelle de 1 2 3 4 5 6   12 pieds

85. Transverse section of card room in the new suite of the Royal Palace.

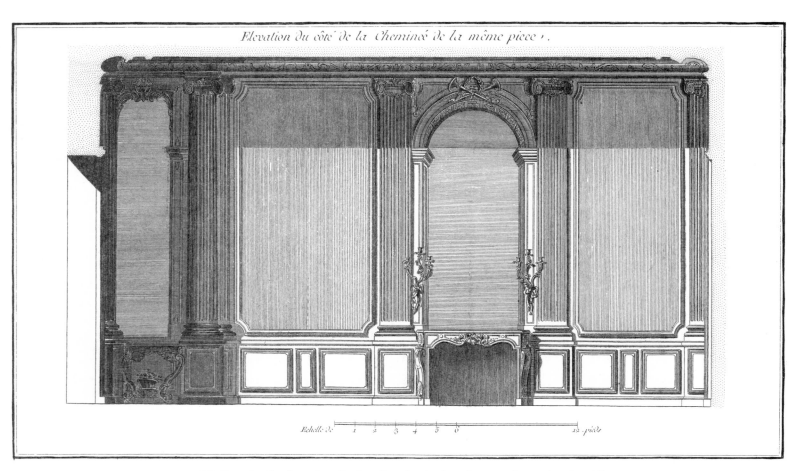

Elevation du côté de la Cheminée de la même piece.

Echelle de 1 2 3 4 5 6   12 pieds

86. Longitudinal section (facing fireplace) of card room shown in plate 85.

54

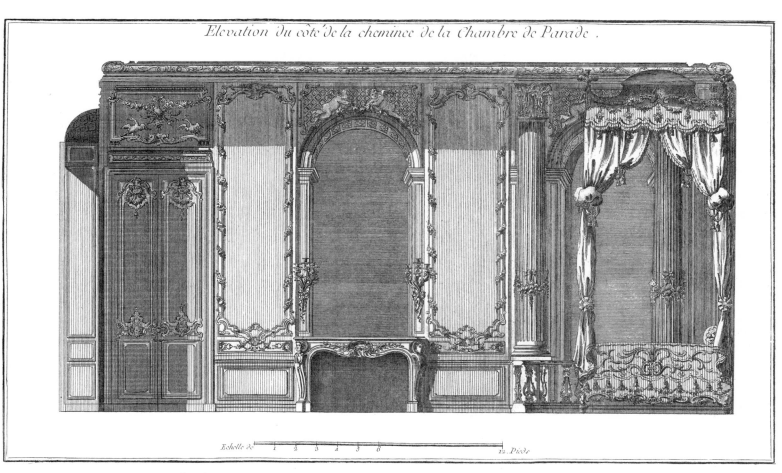

Elevation du côté de la cheminée de la Chambre de Parade.

87. *Longitudinal section (facing fireplace) in Royal audience chamber, new suite of the Royal Palace.*

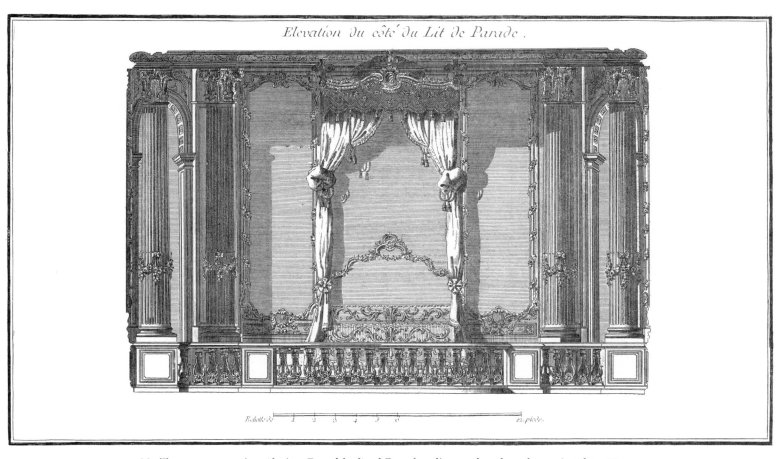

Elevation du côté du Lit de Parade.

88. *Transverse section (facing Royal bed) of Royal audience chamber shown in plate 87.*

Panneaux des Volets de la Chambre
de Parade .

Corniche du Plafond de la Chambre
de Parade .

90. Ornamental details of the Royal audience chamber (plates 87 & 88, above).

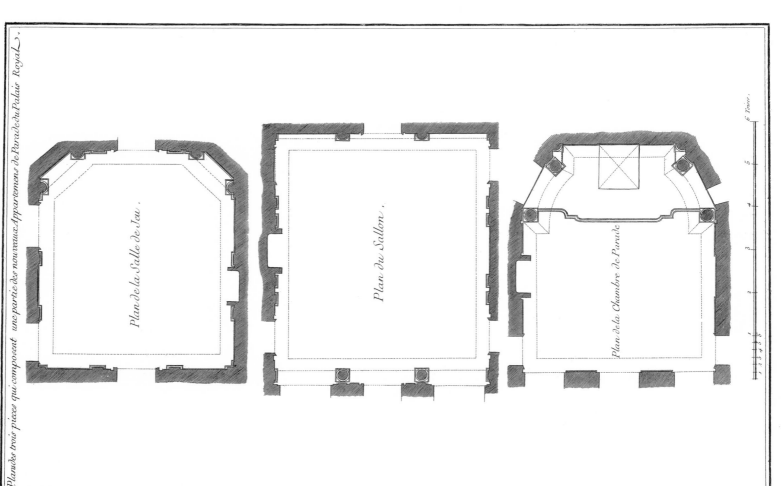

Planches trois pieces qui composent une partie des nouveaux Appartemens de Parade du Palais Royal .

Plan de la Salle de Jeu .

Plan du Sallon .

Plan de la Chambre de Parade

6 Toises .

89. Plans of the three rooms (plates 83–88, above) of the new suite in the Royal Palace.

Developpement des principaux
Ornements répandus dans les
Décorations de trois pièces pré-
sentées.

Dessus de porte de la Chambre de Parade.

Table de marbre et Console placés en face de la cheminée du
Sallon.

Panneaux de la Porte placés dans la chambre de Parade.

Canapé ou Sopha placé dans le Sallon en
face des croisées.

91. Decorative elements of the drawing-room and Royal audience chamber (plates 83, 84, 87 & 88, above).

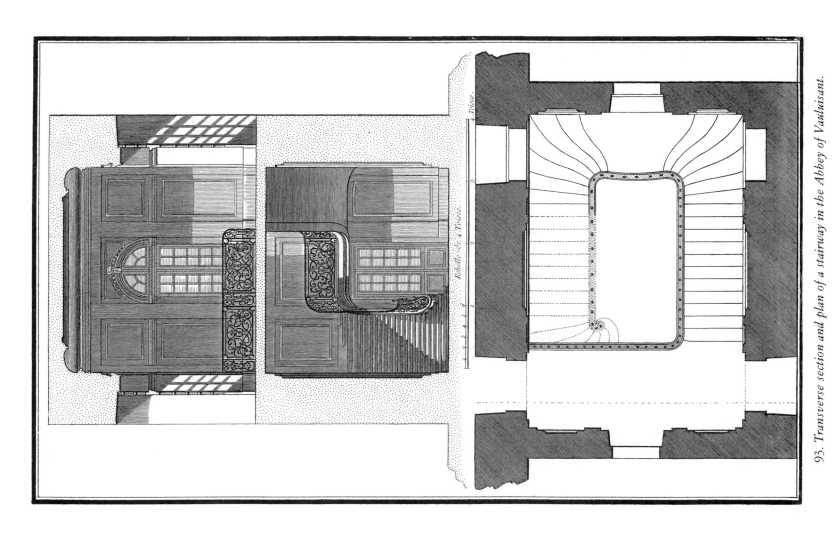

93. *Transverse section and plan of a stairway in the Abbey of Vauluisant.*

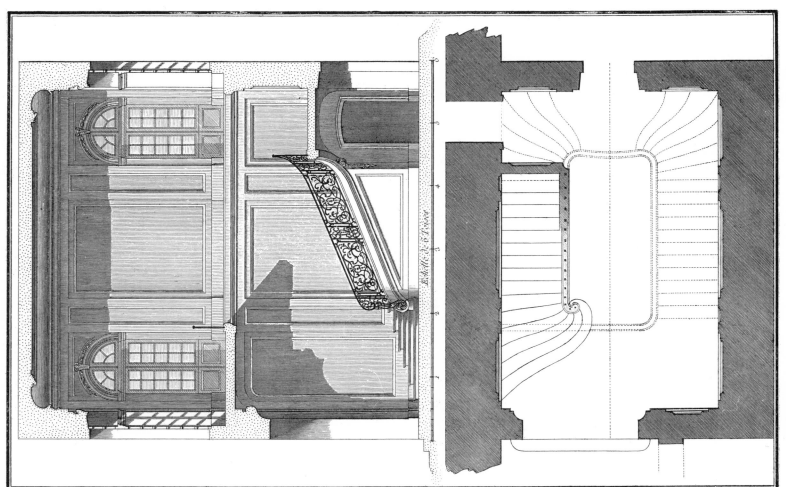

92. *Longitudinal section and plan of a stairway in the Abbey of Vauluisant.*

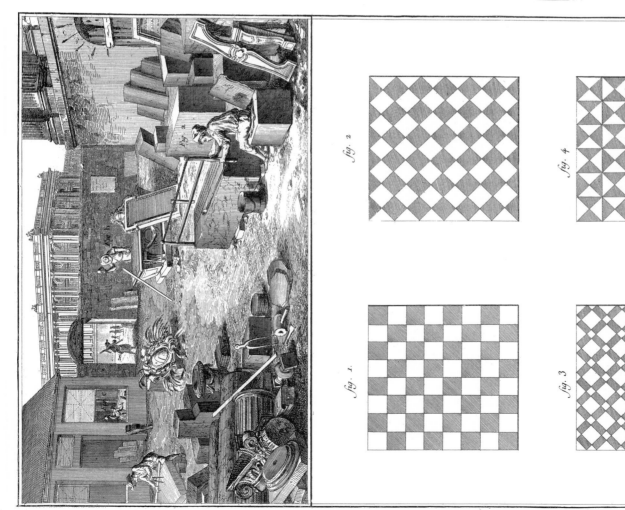

95. *Various marble flooring patterns.*

94. *Marble cutting; various marble flooring patterns.*

59

97. *Marble patterns for hearths of different sizes, and for flooring under vaulted ceilings.*

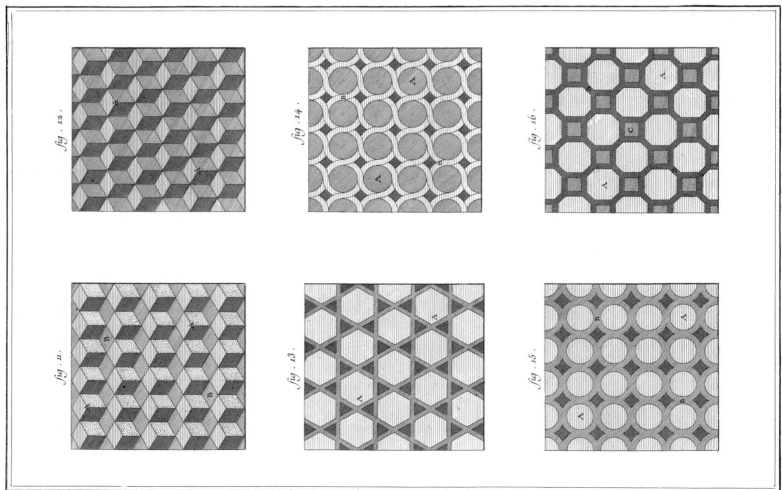

96. *Various marble flooring patterns.*

60

fig . 25 .

fig . 26 .

fig . 27 .

98. Marble flooring patterns for square rooms.

fig . 28 .

fig . 29 .

fig . 30 .

99. Marble flooring patterns for circular rooms.

61

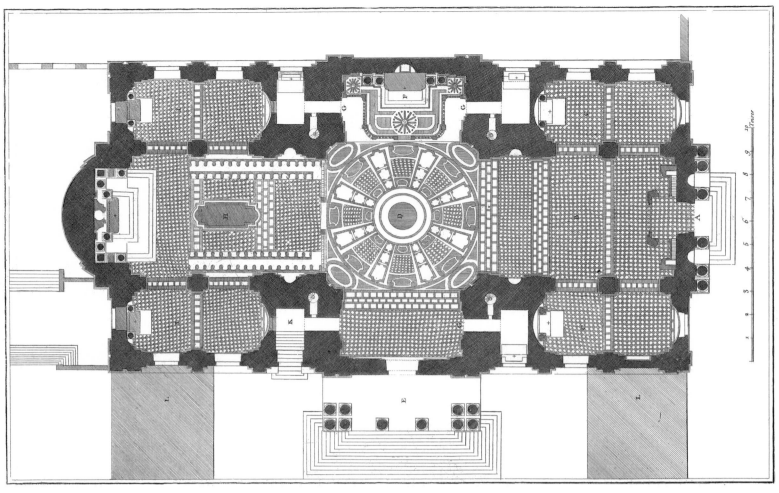

101. *Marble flooring plan of the Church of the Sorbonne, Paris.*

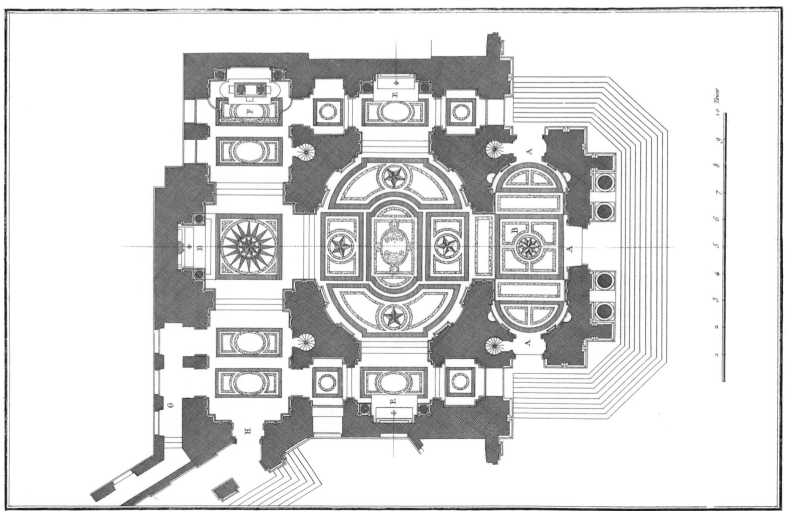

100. *Marble flooring Plan of the Church of the Four Nations, Paris.*

62

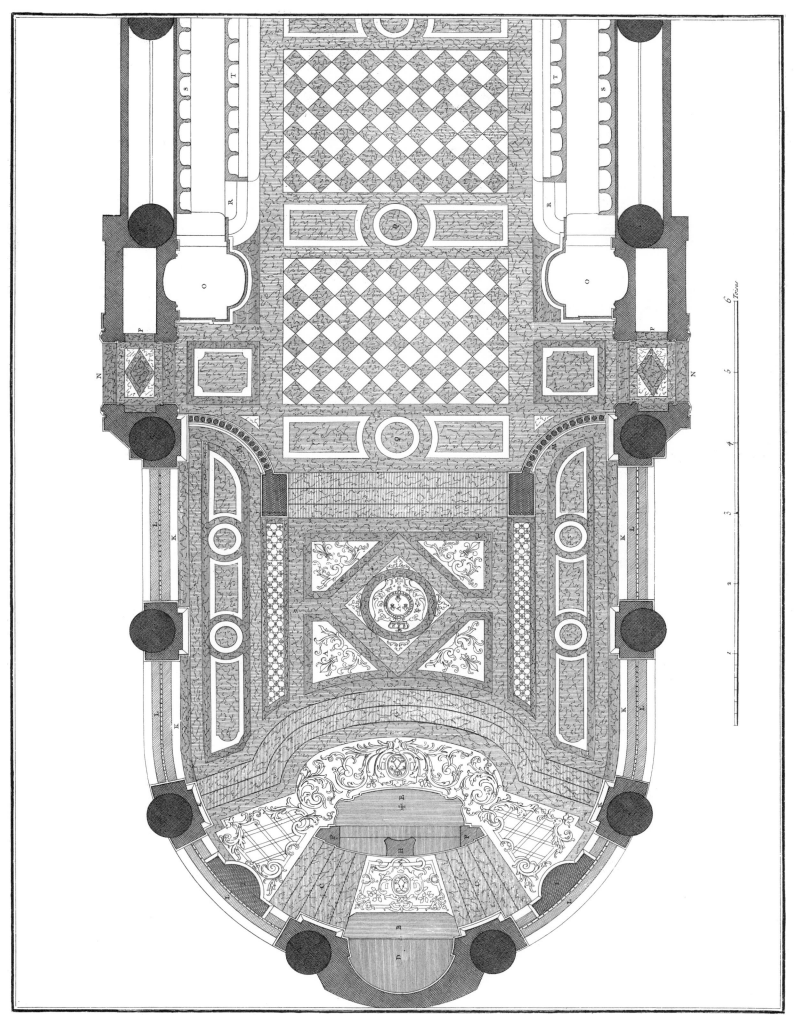

102. *Marble flooring plan of the sanctuary and part of the choir of the Cathedral of Notre-Dame de Paris.*

63

103. *Marble flooring plan of the Church of Val de Grâce, Paris.*

104. *Marble flooring plan of rooms under the Dôme des Invalides, Paris.*

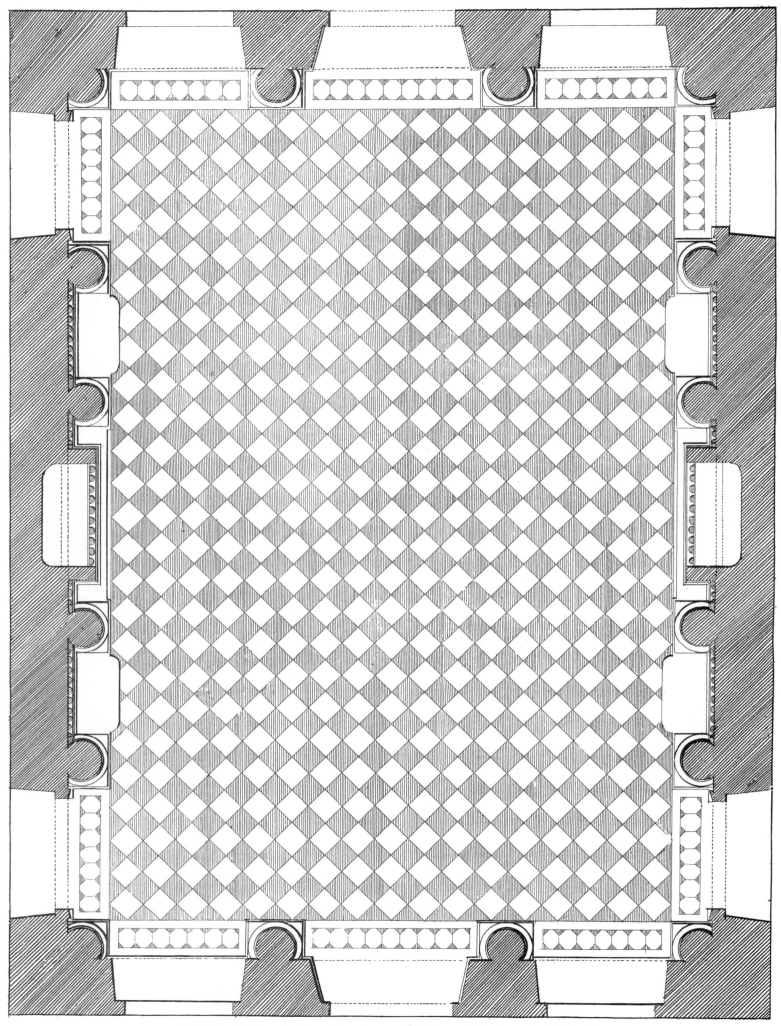

105. *Marble flooring plan of a salon in the Palace of the Marquis de Spinola.*

106. *Ceiling plan of salon shown in plate 105, above.*

107. *Transverse section of salon shown in plates 105 & 106, above.*

108. *Perspective view of salon shown in plates 105–107, above.*

69

110. *Caryatid from the Vatican representing Peace; designed by Raphael.*

109. *Caryatid from the Vatican representing Seafaring; designed by Raphael.*

70

112. *Various caryatids.*

111. *Various caryatids.*

71

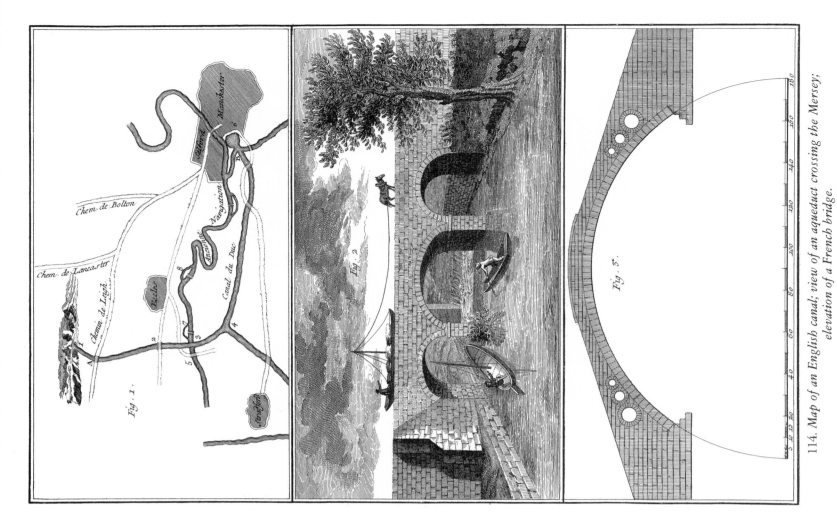

114. *Map of an English canal; view of an aqueduct crossing the Mersey; elevation of a French bridge.*

113. *Various caryatids.*

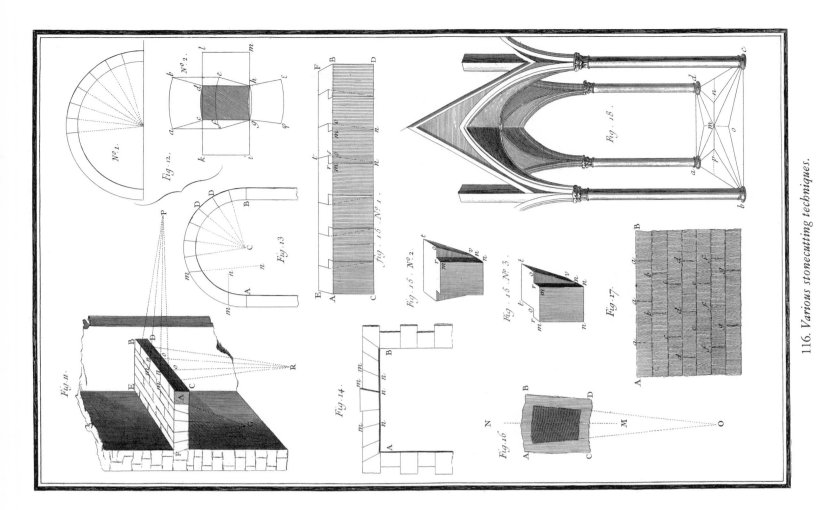

116. *Various stonecutting techniques.*

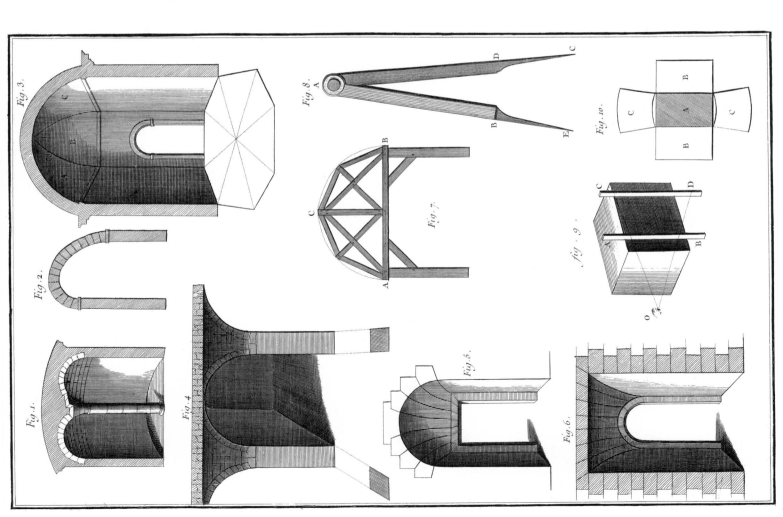

115. *Various cut-stone vaults and arches; stonecutting tools and techniques.*

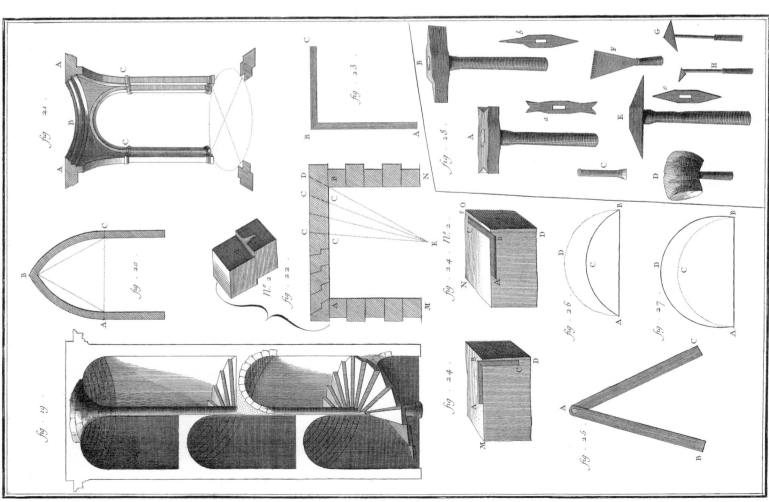

118. *Various stonecutting techniques.*

117. *Various stonecutting techniques and tools.*

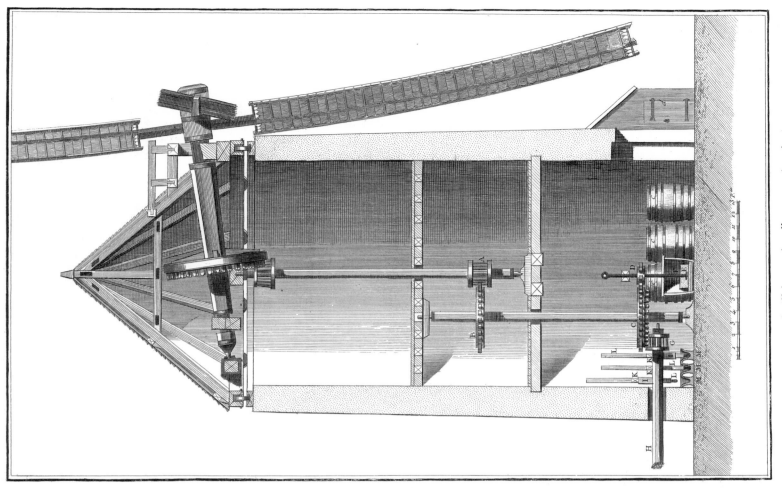

120. *Windmill for sawing flagstones (section).*

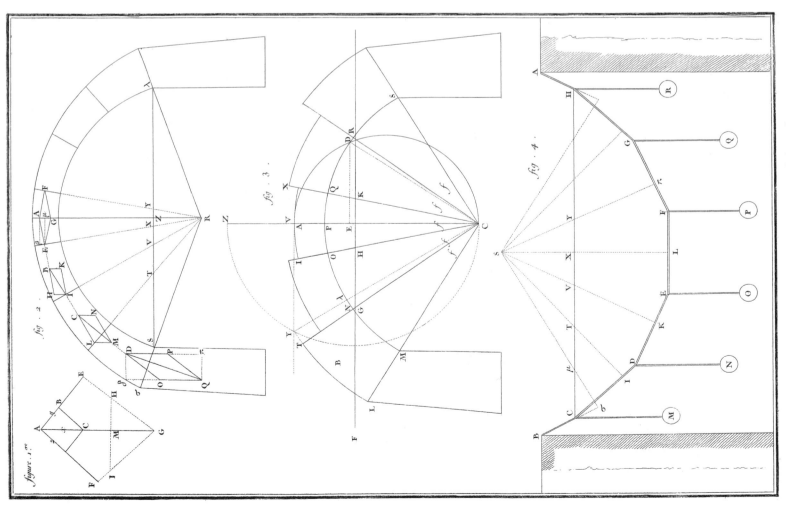

119. *Comparative views of different arches and their thrusts.*

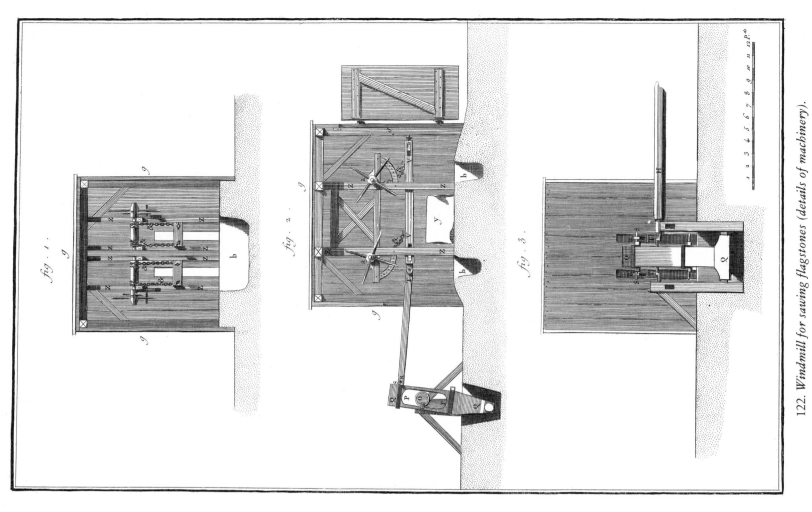

122. *Windmill for sawing flagstones (details of machinery).*

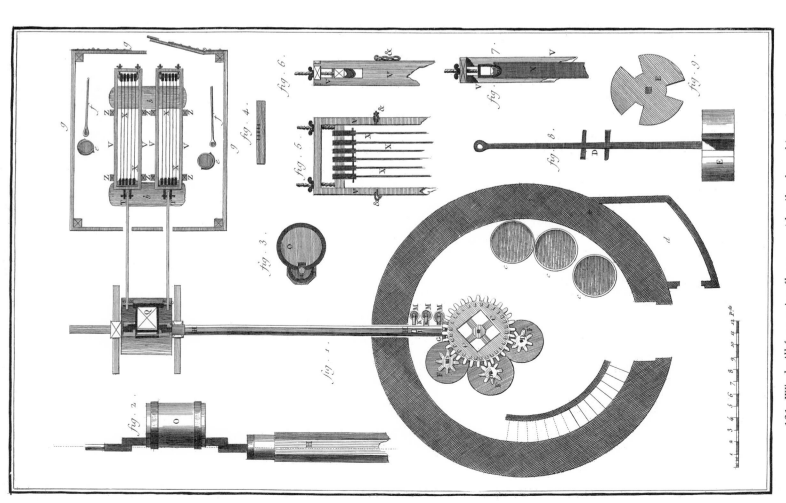

121. *Windmill for sawing flagstones (details of machinery).*

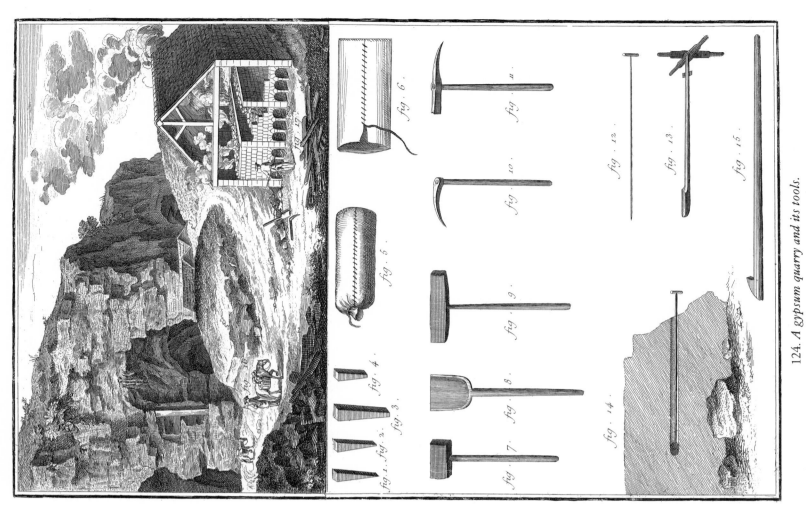

124. A gypsum quarry and its tools.

123. Machinery for drilling stone and turning columns.

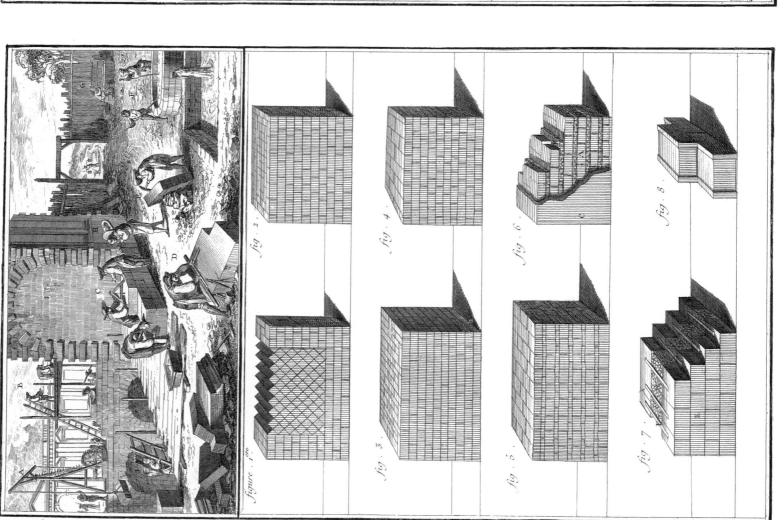

126. *Various bricklaying patterns (continued).*

125. *Masons at work and various bricklaying patterns.*

78

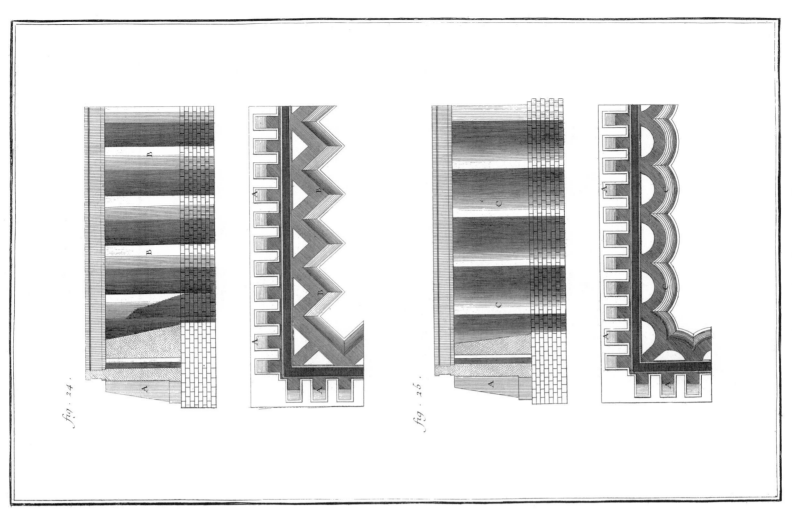

128. *Construction of terrace walls.*

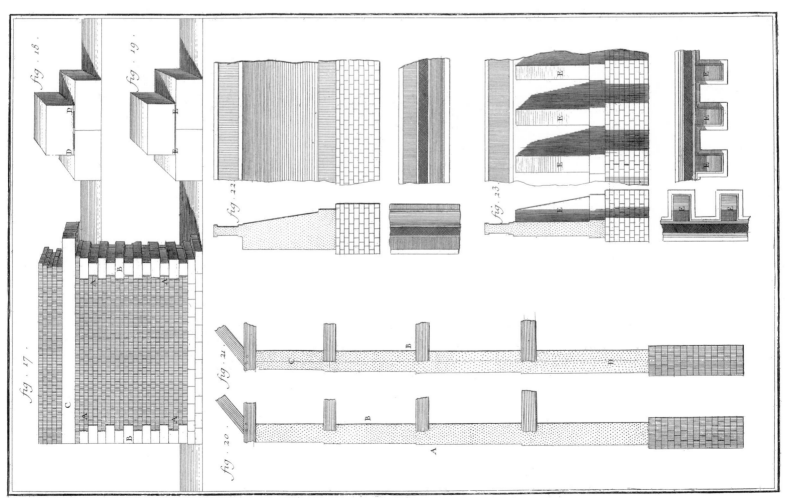

127. *Construction of facade and terrace walls.*

79

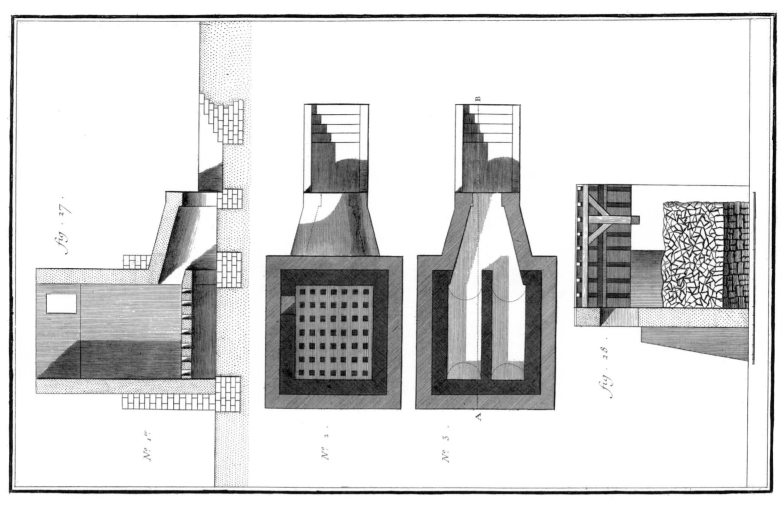

130. Section and plans of a brick and tile kiln; longitudinal section of a plaster kiln.

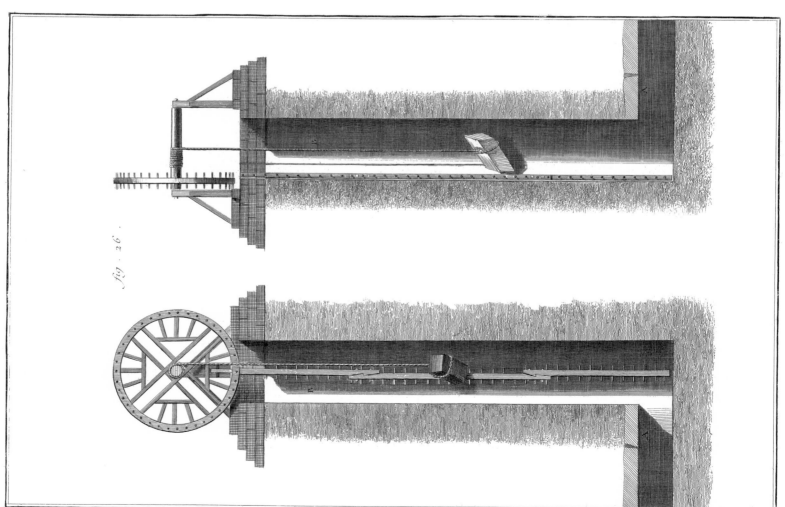

129. Perpendicular views of a quarry entrance.

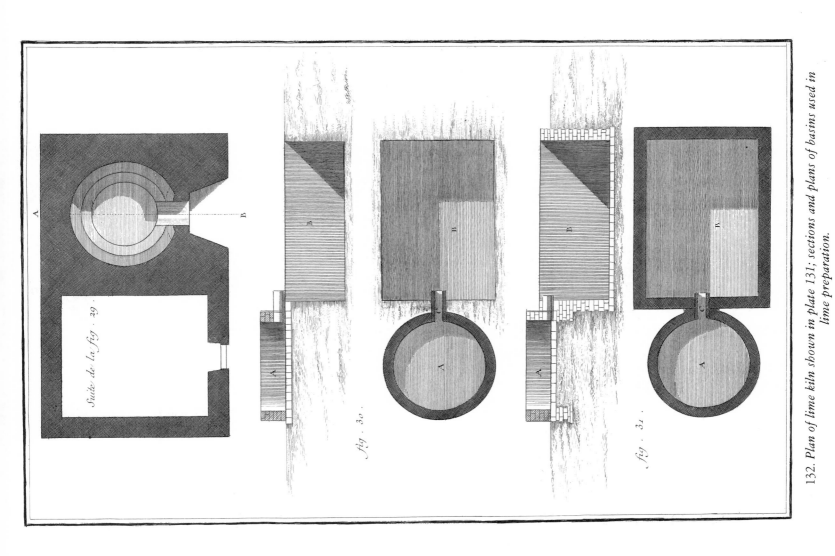

132. Plan of lime kiln shown in plate 131; sections and plans of basins used in lime preparation.

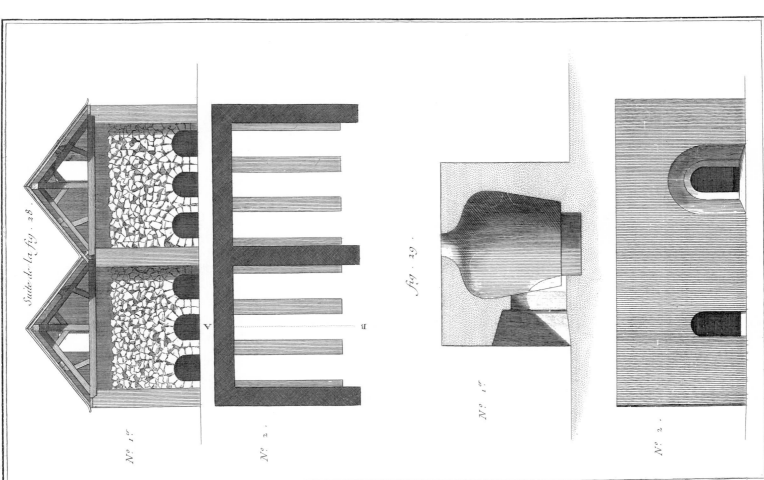

131. Transverse section and plan of plaster kiln shown in plate 130, above; longitudinal section and elevation of a lime kiln.

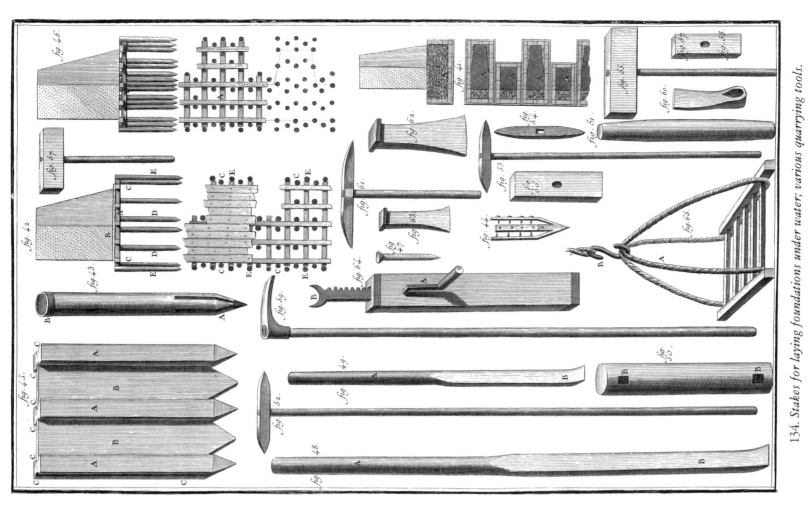

134. Stakes for laying foundations under water; various quarrying tools.

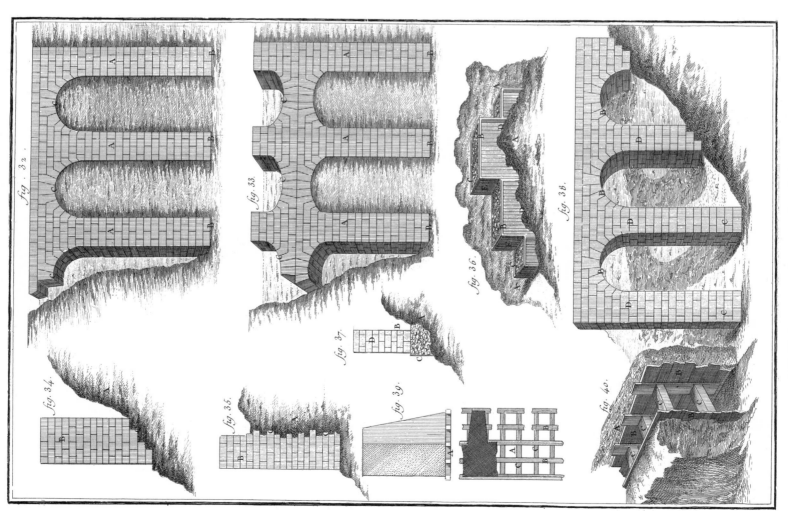

133. Various types of masonry foundations.

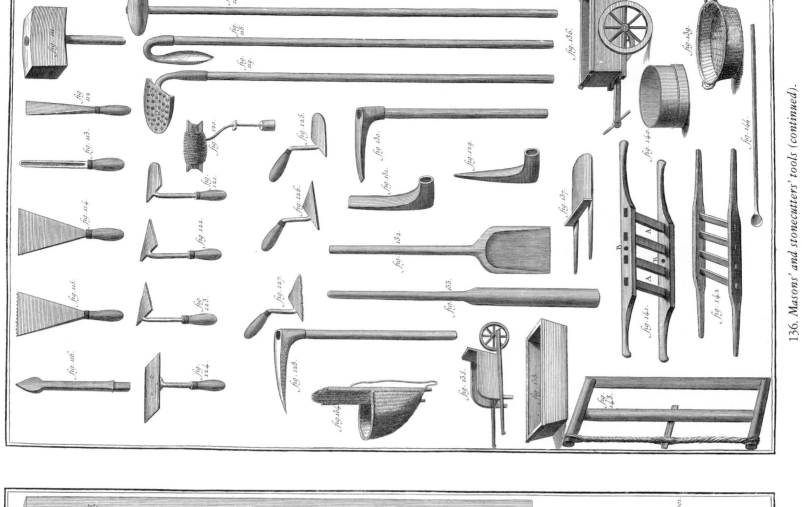

136. Masons' and stonecutters' tools (continued).

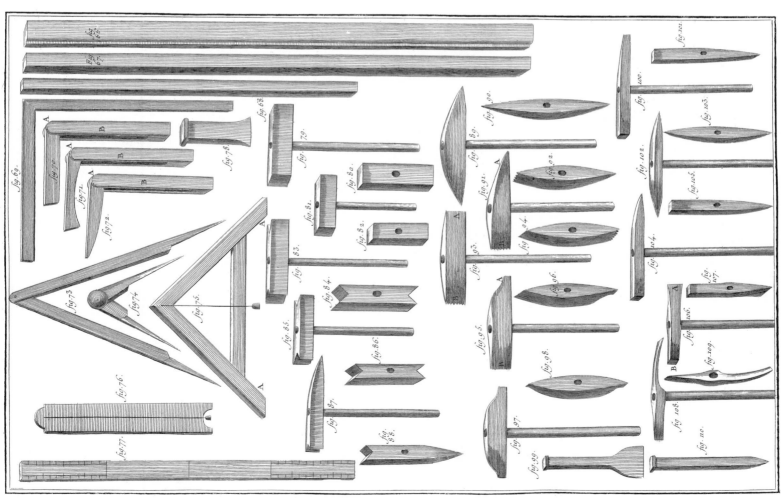

135. Masons' and stonecutters' tools.

83

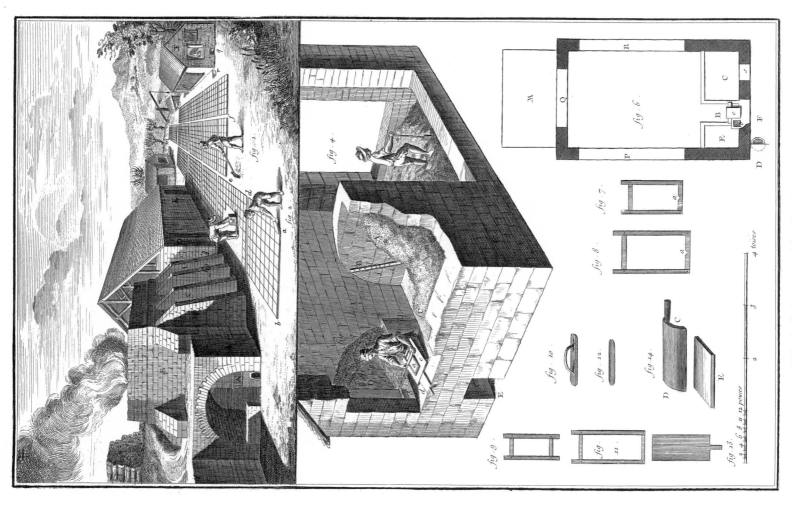

138. *A tile factory and details of tilemaking.*

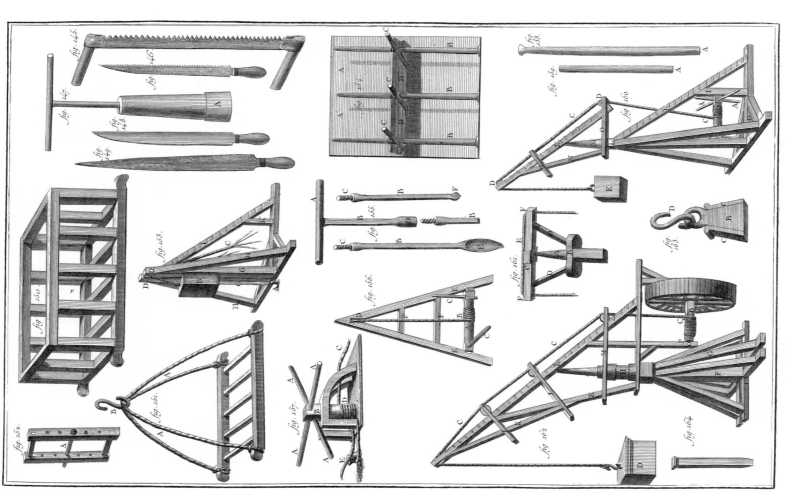

137. *Masons' and stonecutters' tools (continued).*

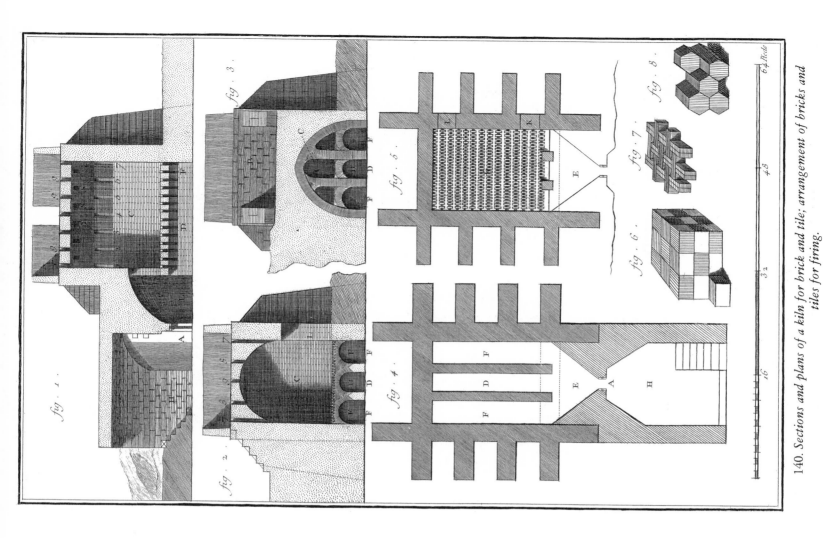

140. Sections and plans of a kiln for brick and tile; arrangement of bricks and tiles for firing.

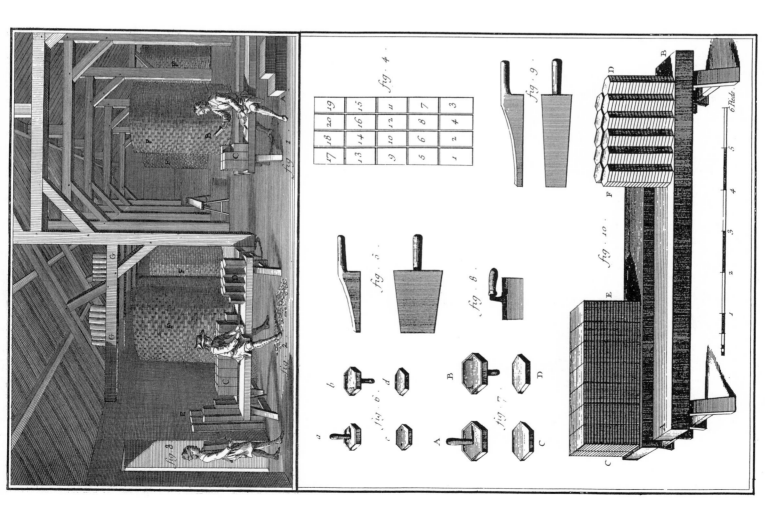

139. Cutting hexagonal flooring tiles.

85

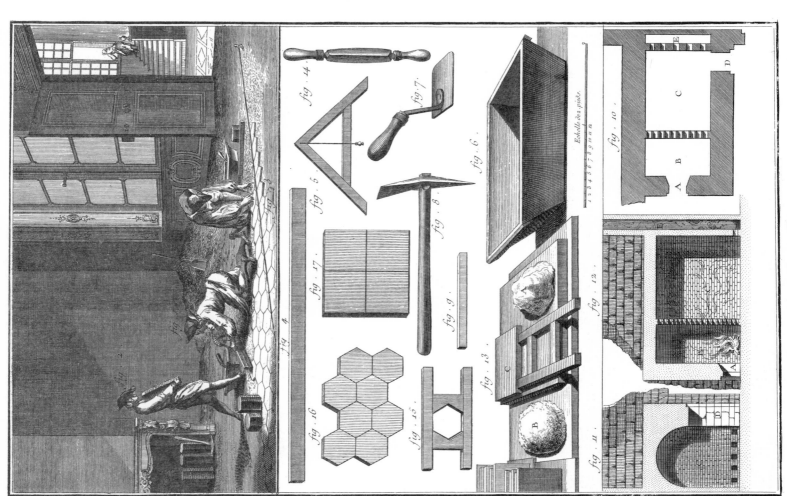

141. Laying floor tile; floor-tilers' implements and patterns; plan and sections of a tile-kiln.

142. Table showing 64 different orientations for a pair of two-colored tiles.

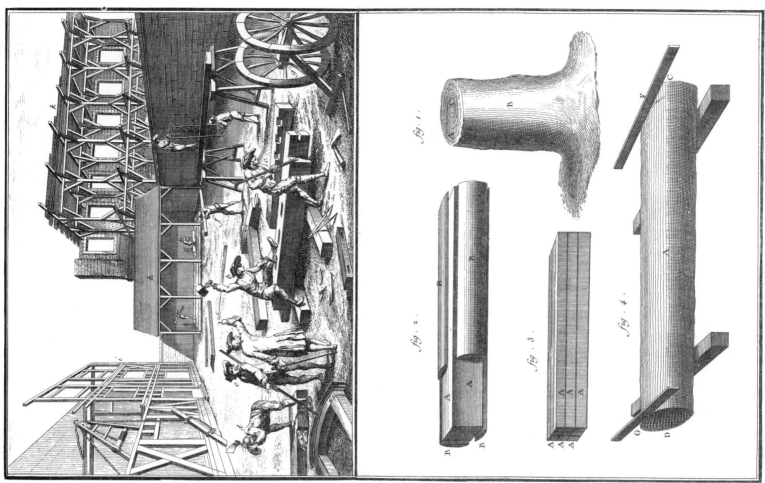

144. Wood-frame construction; methods of hewing logs.

143. Laying roof tile; roof-tilers' tools.

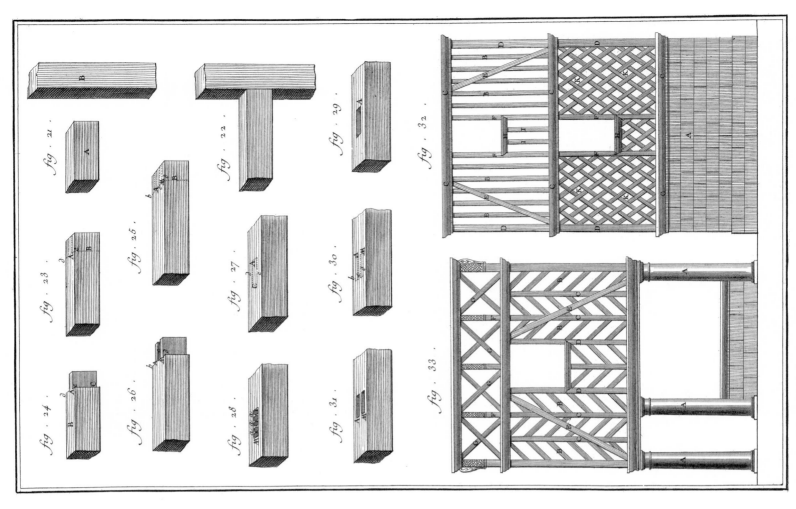

146. *Method of cutting tenons and mortises; two former methods of framing walls.*

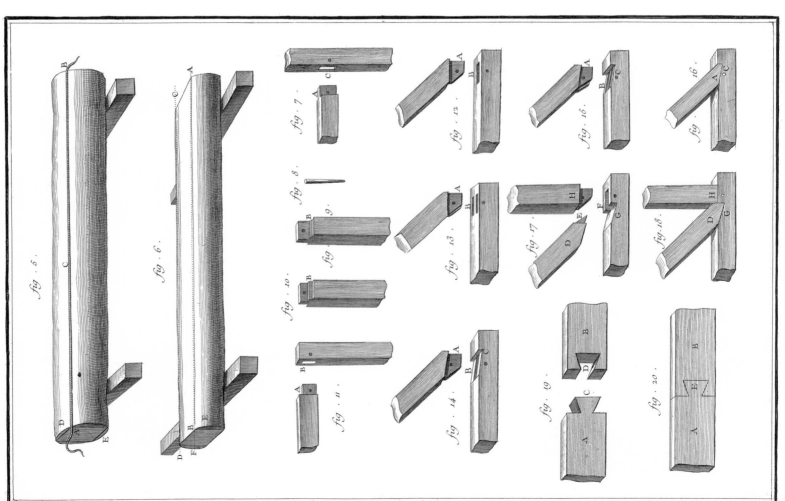

145. *Methods of hewing logs (continued); various wood joints.*

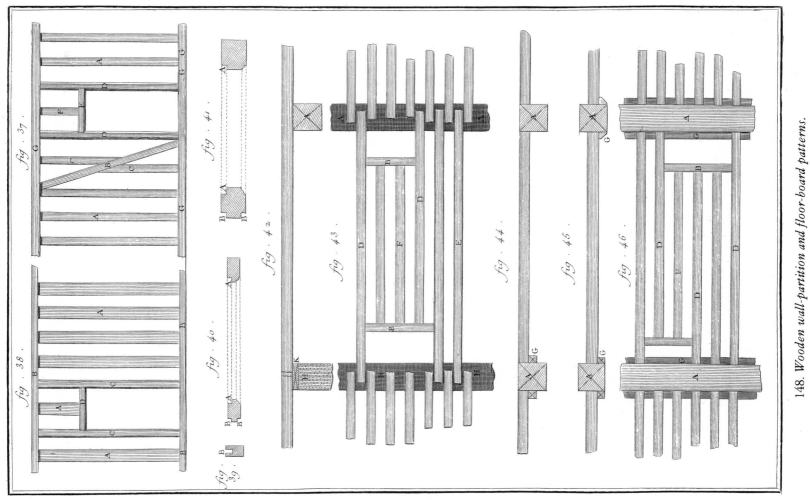

148. Wooden wall-partition and floor-board patterns.

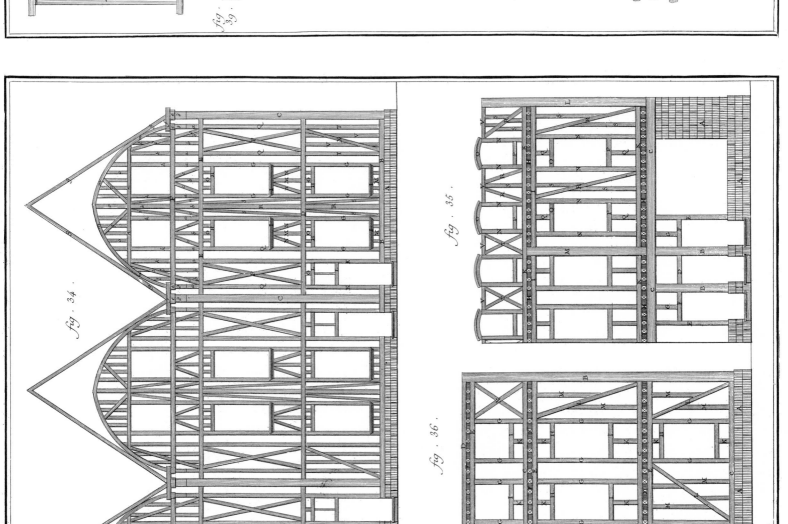

147. A wall-framing method of around 150 years previous [circa 1600]; two modern wall-framing methods.

89

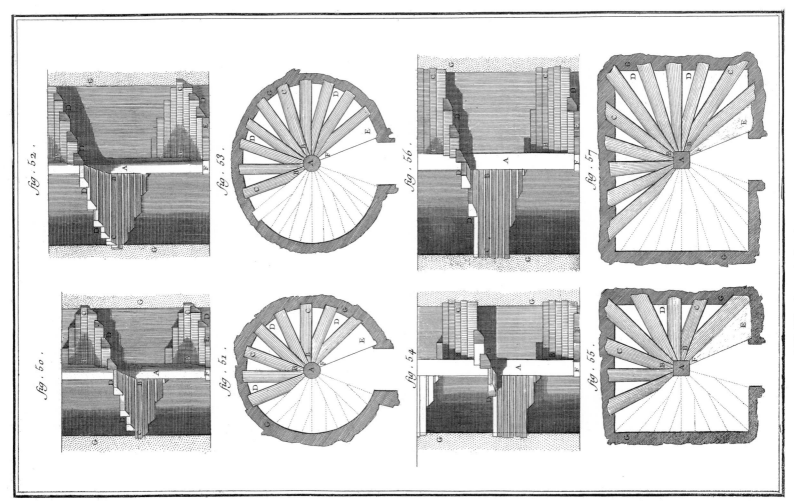

150. Wooden spiral staircase patterns.

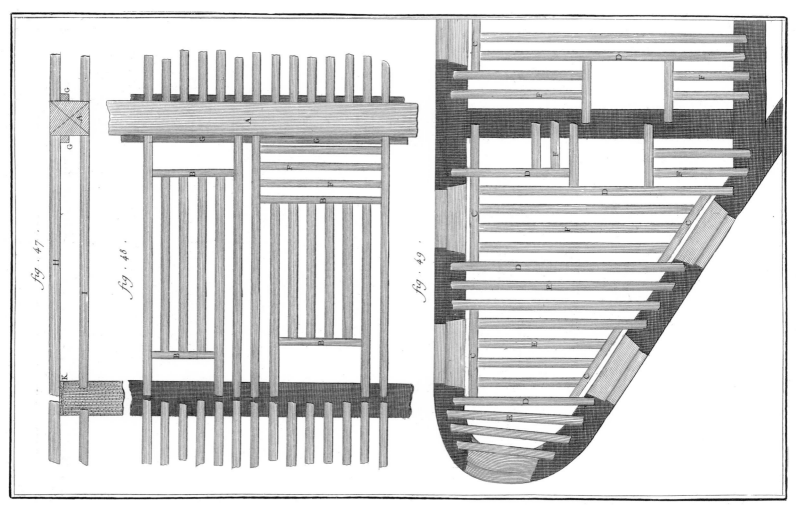

149. Floor-board patterns (continued).

90

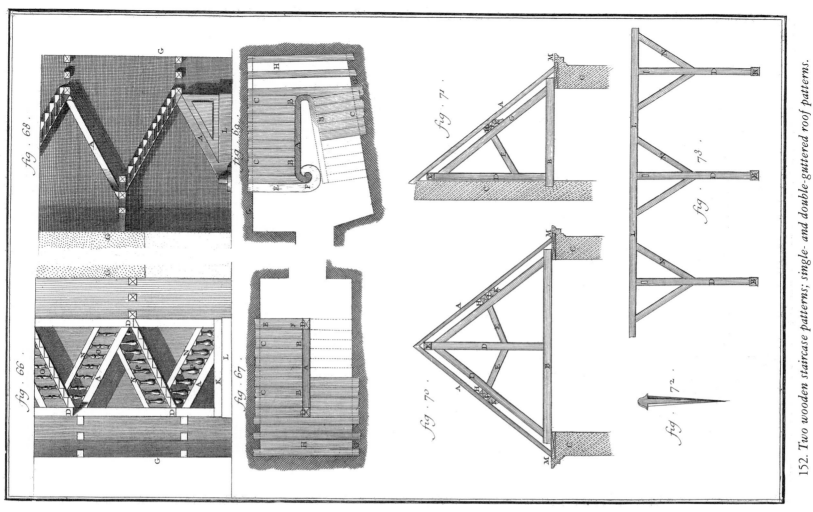

152. Two wooden staircase patterns; single- and double-guttered roof patterns.

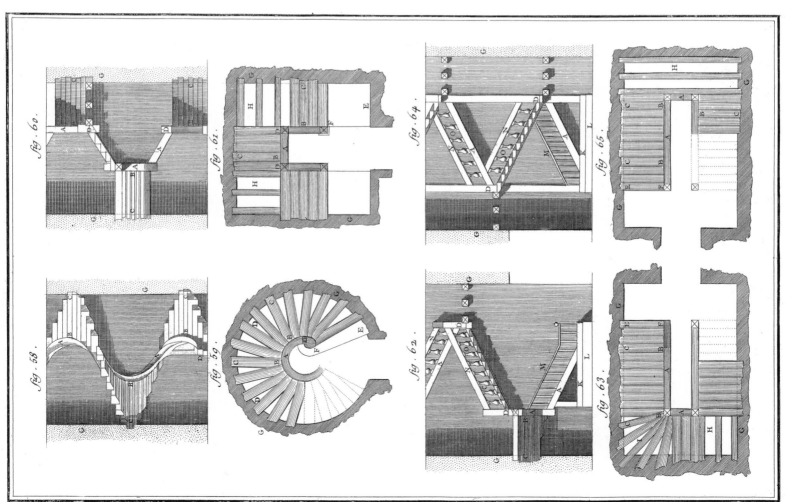

151. Wooden winding and other staircase patterns.

91

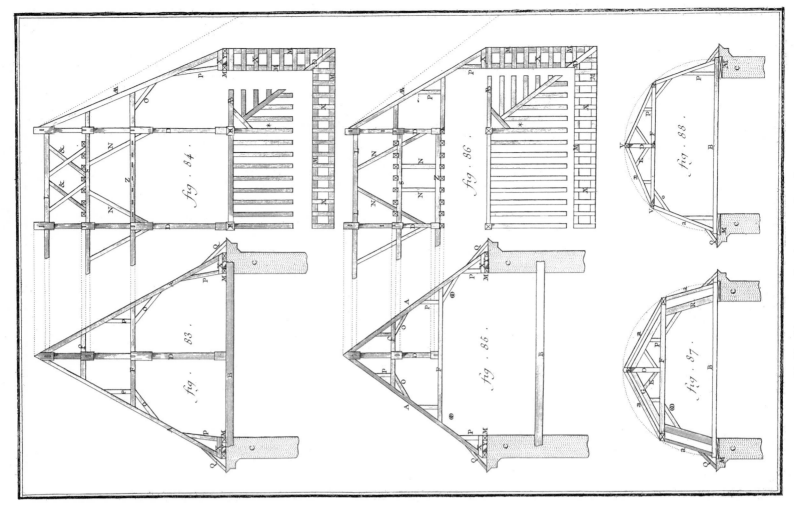

154. *Double-guttered and mansard roof patterns.*

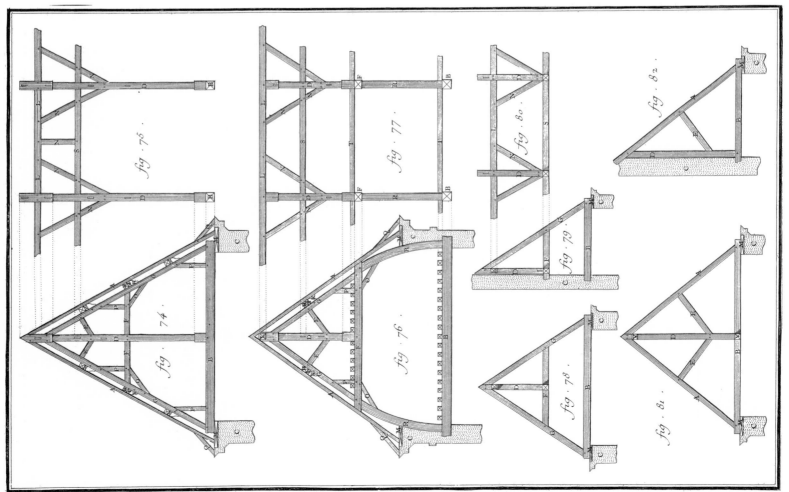

153. *Single- and double-guttered roof patterns (continued).*

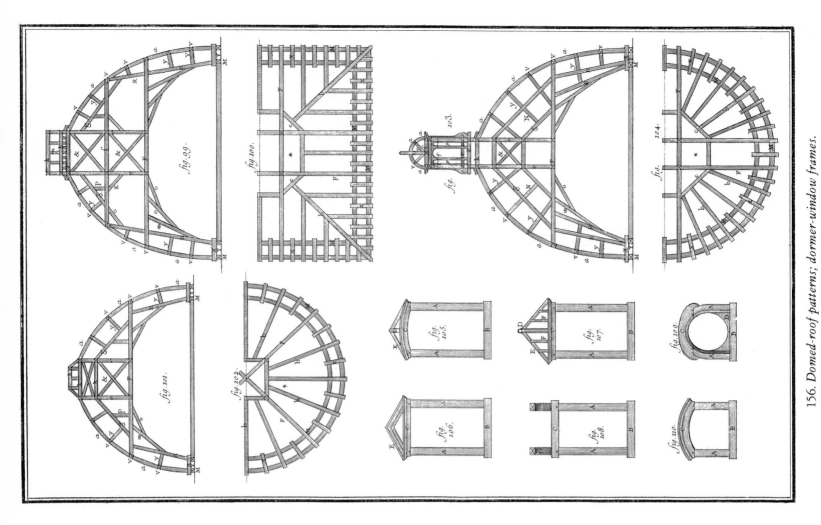

156. *Domed-roof patterns; dormer-window frames.*

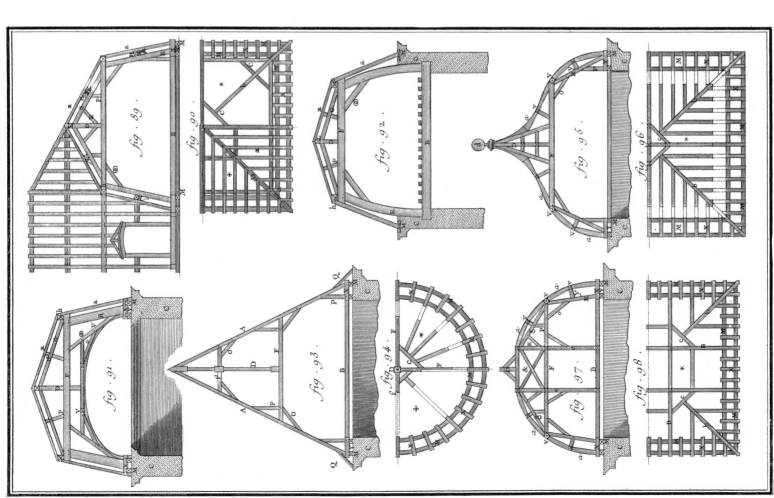

155. *Various roof patterns.*

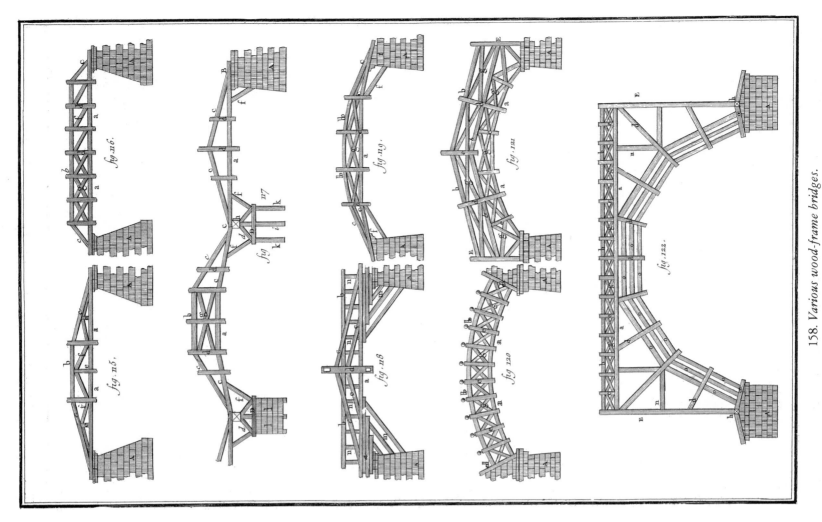

158. Various wood-frame bridges.

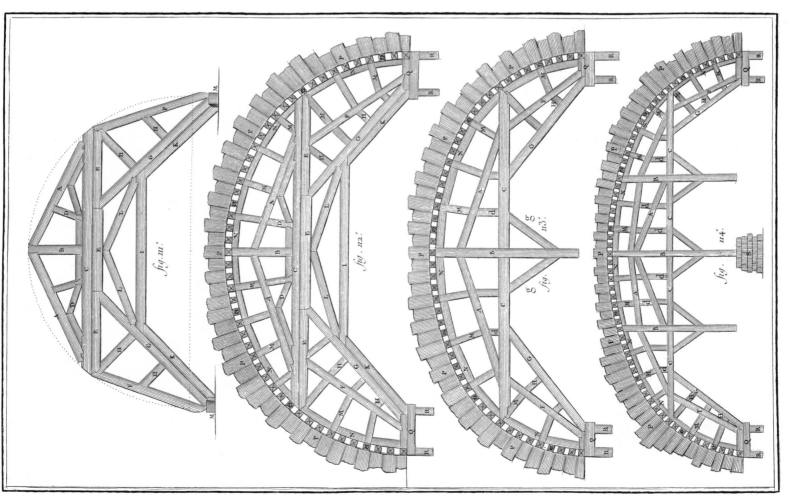

157. Various roof trusses.

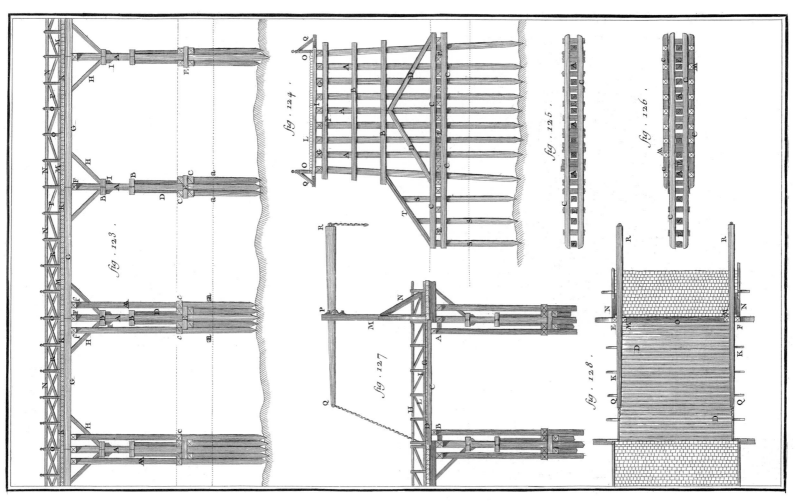

fig. 129.

fig. 130.

fig. 131.

fig. 132.

fig. 133.

160. A sliding bridge and a swing bridge.

fig. 123.

fig. 124.

fig. 125.

fig. 126.

fig. 127.

fig. 128.

159. A large bridge and a drawbridge.

162. *Laying a foundation on piles.*

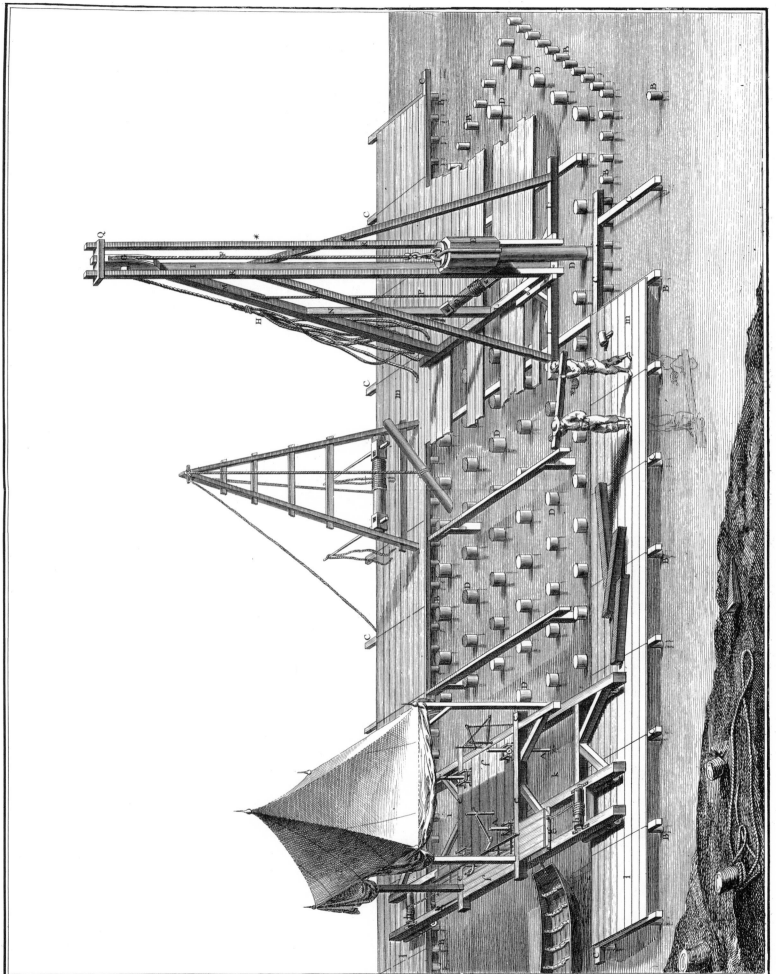

163. *Above-water view of an underwater saw (under tent at left) and a pile driver.*

164. Mechanism of underwater saw shown in plate 163, above.

165. *Large casing for containing foundations on piles.*

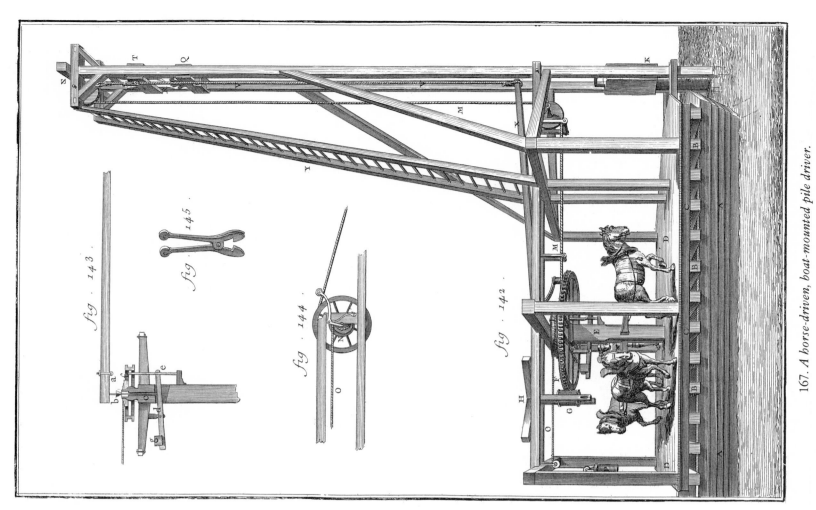

167. A horse-driven, boat-mounted pile driver.

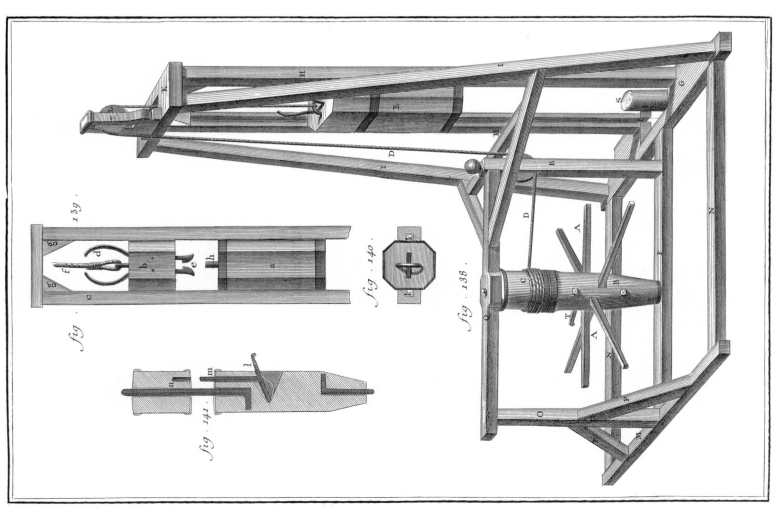

166. A pile driver.

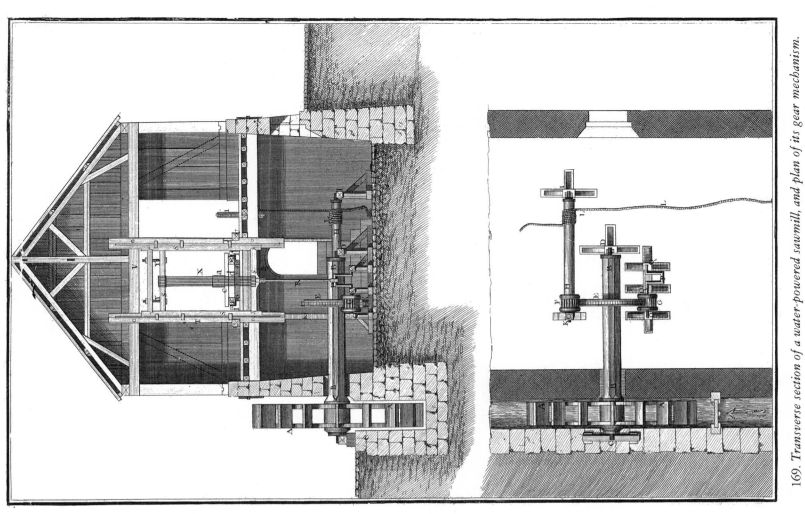

169. Transverse section of a water-powered sawmill, and plan of its gear mechanism.

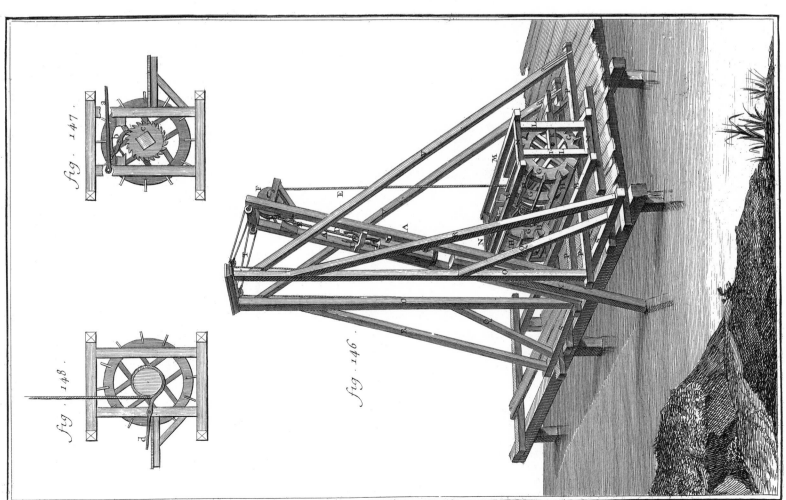

168. An obliquely oriented pile driver.

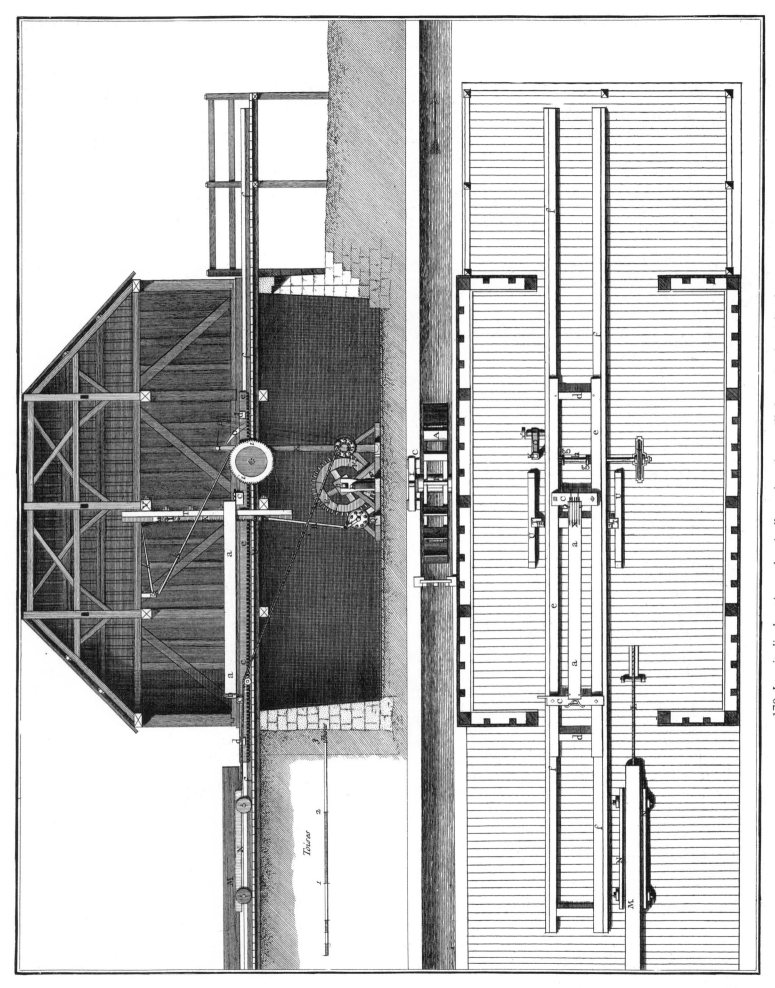

170. *Longitudinal section and main-floor plan of sawmill shown in plate 169, above.*

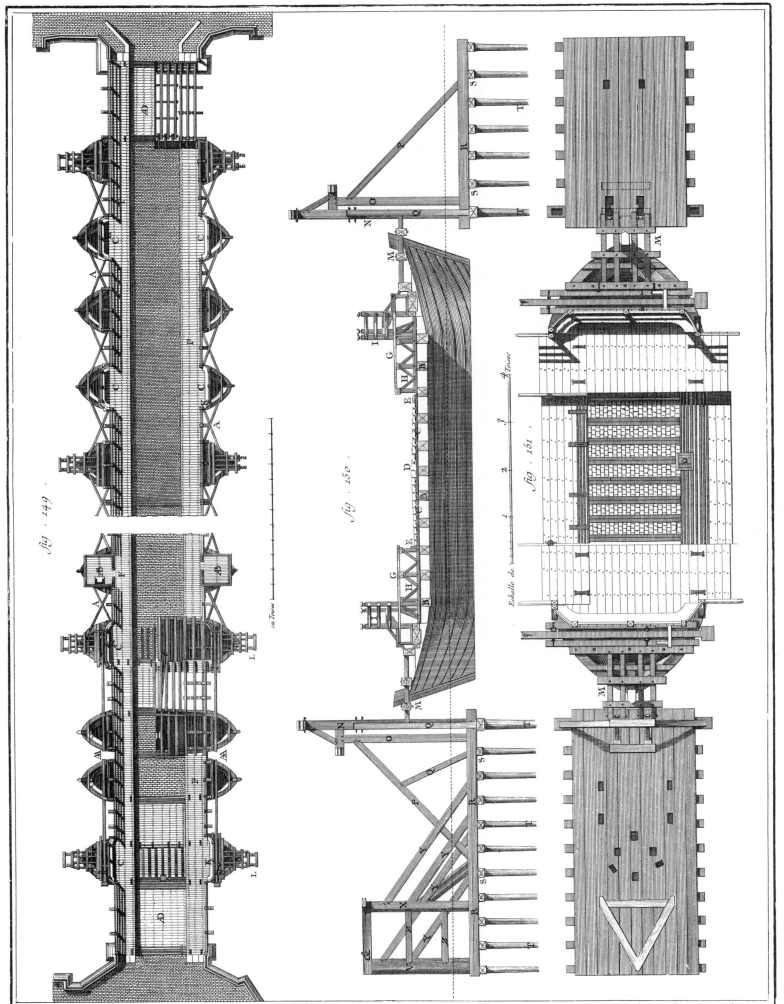

171. *View of a pontoon bridge built over the Seine at Rouen, and two views of its construction.*

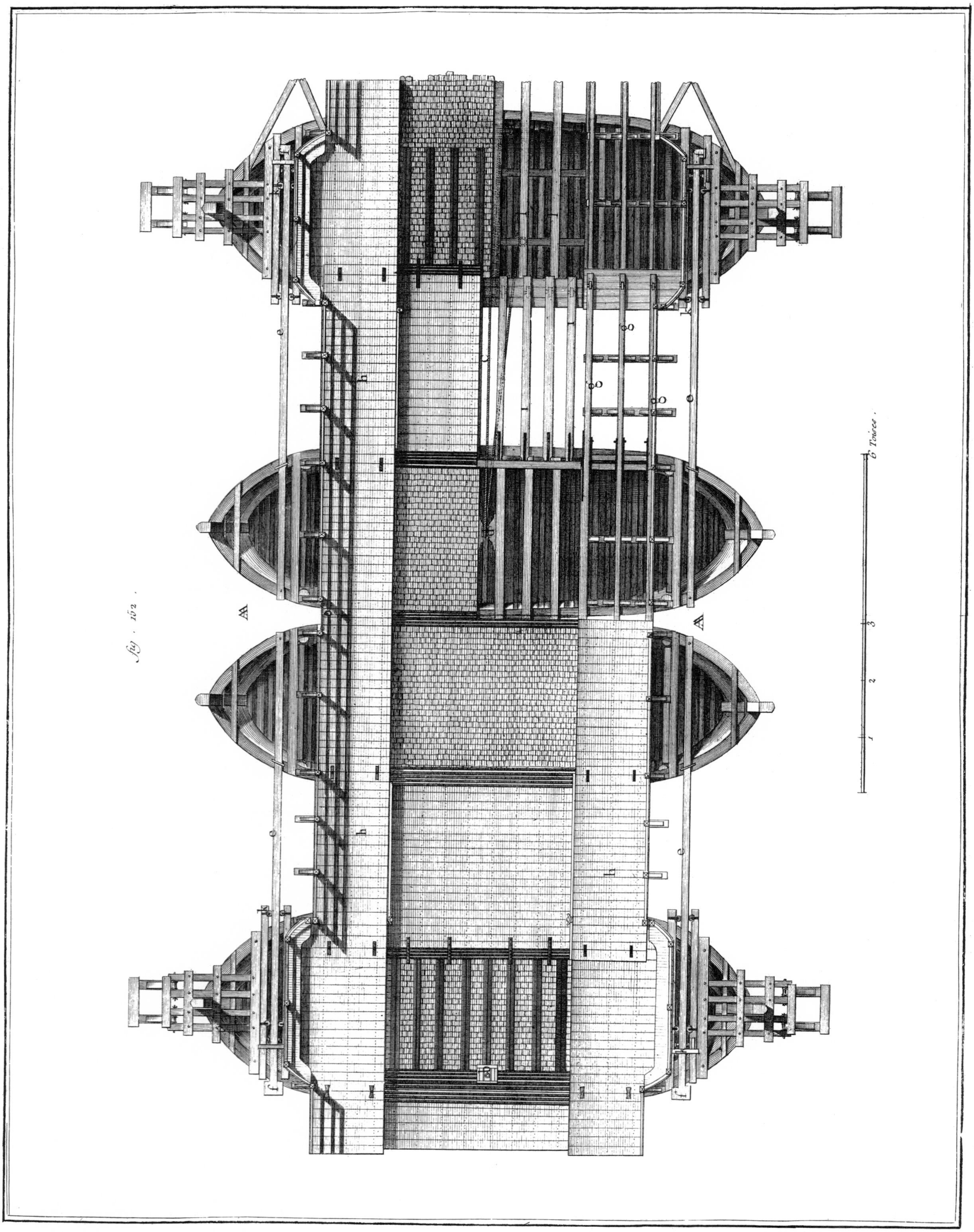

fig. 172.

172. Cutaway view of the pontoon bridge shown in plate 171, above.

173. *Plan of the water-pump of the Notre-Dame Bridge, Paris.*

174. *Longitudinal section, water-pump of the Notre-Dame Bridge.*

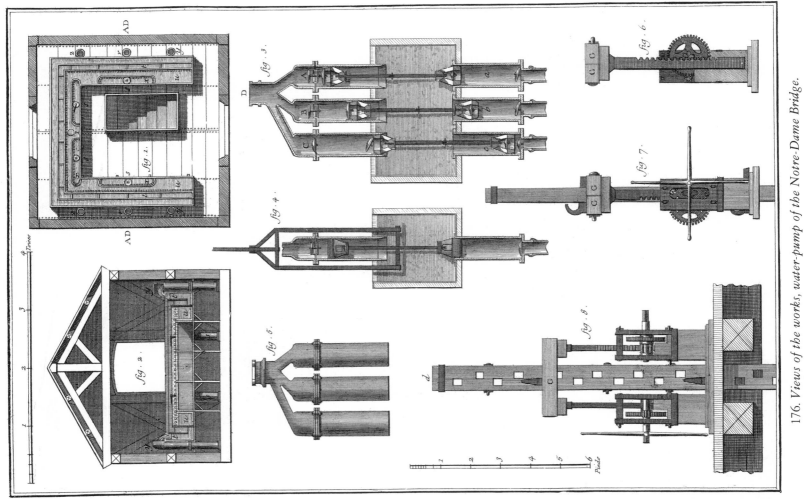

176. *Views of the works, water-pump of the Notre-Dame Bridge.*

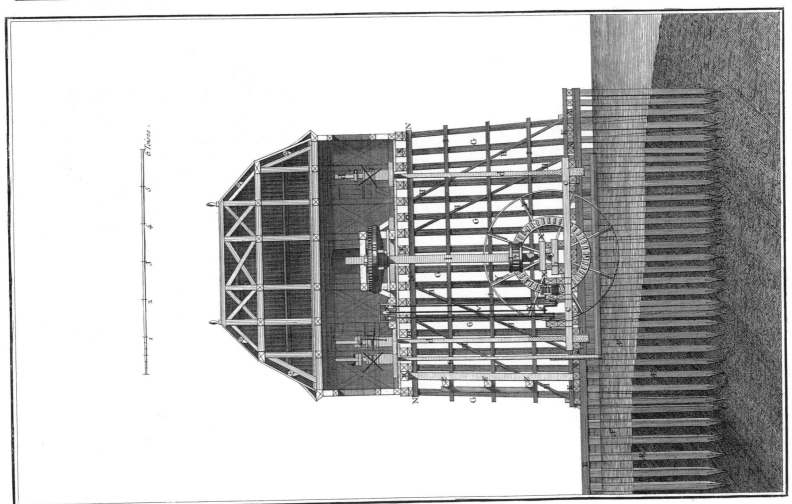

175. *Transverse section, water-pump of the Notre-Dame Bridge.*

107

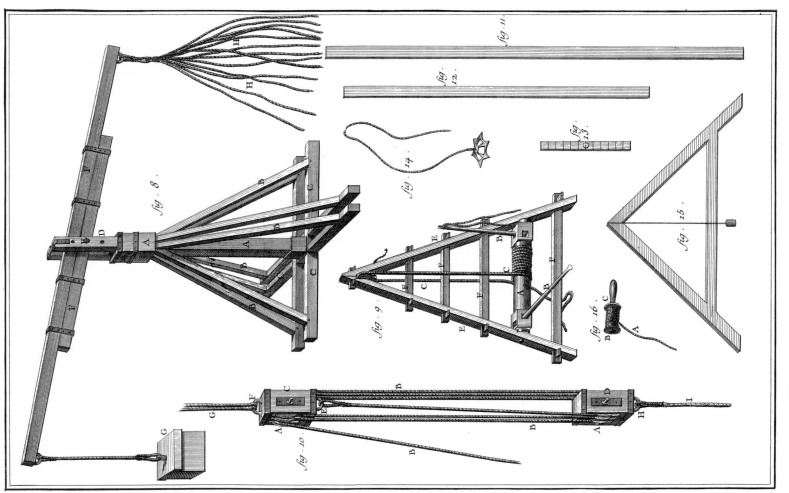

178. Carpenters' tools (continued): bascule, gin, tackle, etc.

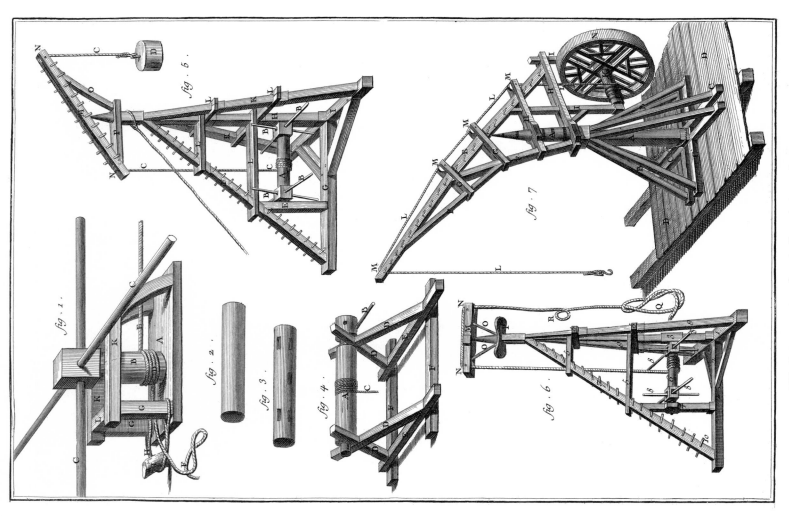

177. Carpenters' tools: windlass, hoist and cranes.

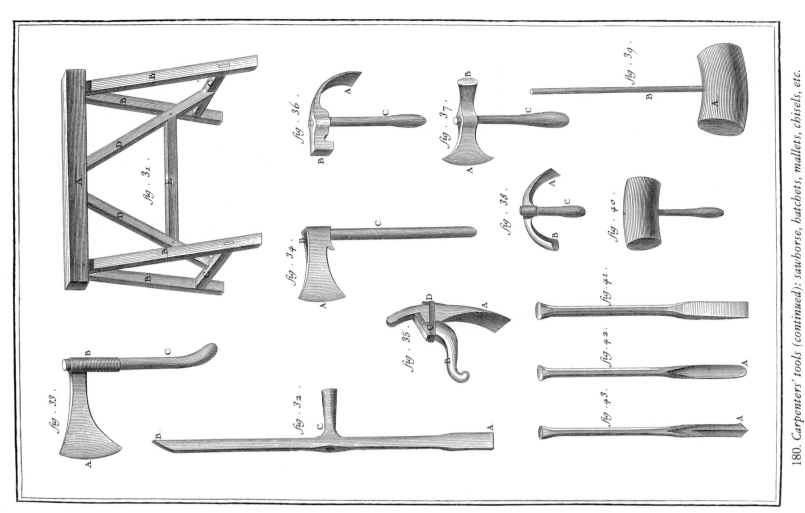

180. *Carpenters' tools (continued): sawhorse, hatchets, mallets, chisels, etc.*

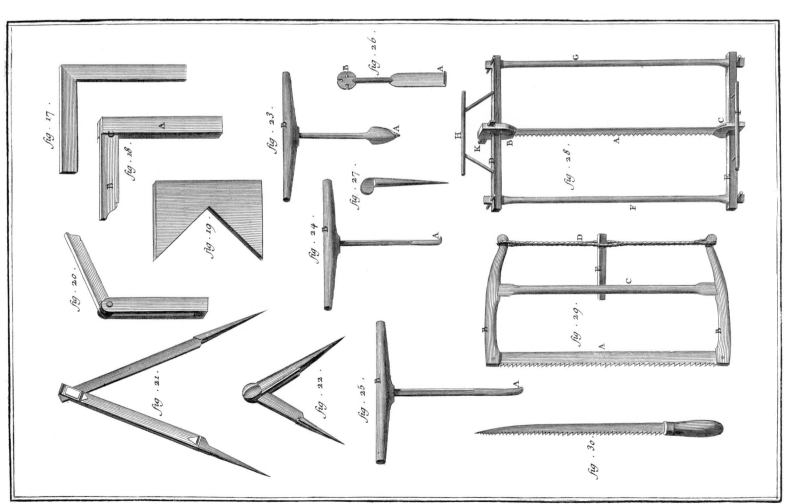

179. *Carpenters' tools (continued): squares, compasses, augers, saws, etc.*

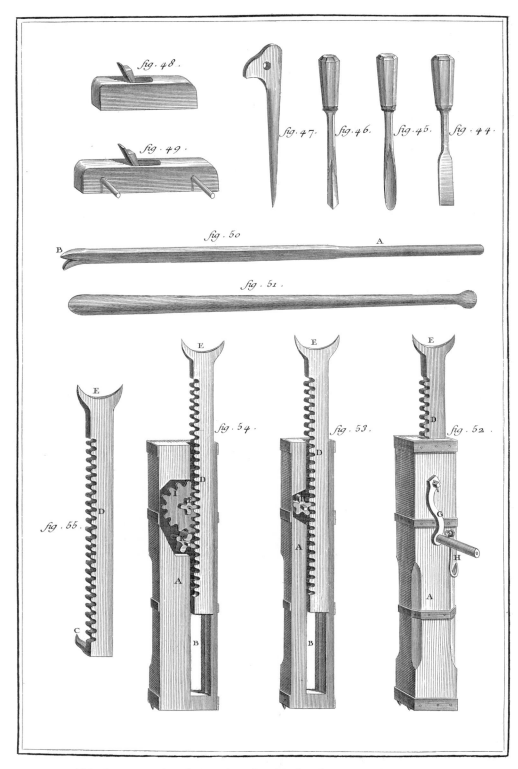

181. *Carpenters' tools (continued): chisels, planes, crowbar, jack, etc.*

APPENDIX

The following is a listing of the classification and placement of the plates in the original *Encyclopédie:*

1. Architecture, I.
2. Architecture, II.
3. Architecture, III.
4. Architecture, IV.
5. Architecture, V.
6. Architecture, VI.
7. Architecture, VII.
8. Architecture, VIII.
9. Architecture, IX.
10. Architecture, X.
11. Architecture, XI.
12. Architecture, XII.
13. Architecture Supplement, 1.
14. Architecture Supplement, 2.
15. Architecture Supplement, 3.
16. Architecture Supplement, 4.
17. Architecture Supplement, 5.
18. Architecture Supplement, 6.
19. Architecture Supplement, 7.
20. Architecture Supplement, 8.
21. Architecture Supplement, 9.
22. Architecture Supplement, 10.
23. Architecture Supplement, 11.
24. Architecture, XIV.
25. Architecture, XIII.
26. Architecture, XV.
27. Architecture, XVI.
28. Architecture, XVII.
29. Architecture, XVIII.
30. Architecture, XIX.
31. Architecture, XX.
32. Architecture, XXI.
33. Architecture Supplement (Bagne de Brest), Pl. 3, No. 2.
34. Architecture Supplement (Bagne de Brest), Pl. 1 & Pl. 2.
35. Architecture Supplement (Bagne de Brest), following Pl. 2/3.
36. Architecture, XXII.
37. Architecture, XXIII.
38. Architecture, XXIV.
39. Architecture, XXV.
40. Architecture, XXVI.
41. Architecture, XXVII.
42. Architecture, XXVIII.
43. Théatres, B.
44. Théatres, C.
45. Théatres, D.
46. Théatres, E.
47. Théatres, F.
48. Théatres, G.
49. Théatres, H.
50. Théatres, I.
51. Théatres, K.
52. Théatres, L.
53. Théatres, A.
54. Théatres, Q.
55. Théatres, M.
56. Théatres, N.
57. Théatres, O.
58. Théatres, P.
59. Théatres, R.
60. Théatres, S.
61. Théatres, T.
62. Théatres, V.
63. Théatres, X.
64. Théatres, Y.
65. Architecture (Théatres) Supplement, A.
66. Architecture (Théatres) Supplement, B.
67. Architecture (Théatres) Supplement, C.
68. Architecture (Théatres) Supplement, D.
69. Architecture (Théatres) Supplement, F.
70. Architecture (Théatres) Supplement, G.
71. Architecture (Théatres) Supplement, H.
72. Architecture (Théatres) Supplement, E.
73. Architecture (Théatres) Supplement, I.
74. Théatres, Z.
75. Théatres, &.
76. Théatres, AA.
77. Théatres, GG.
78. Théatres, BB.
79. Théatres, CC.
80. Théatres, DD.
81. Théatres, EE.
82. Théatres, FF.
83. Architecture, XXIX.
84. Architecture, XXX.
85. Architecture, XXXI.
86. Architecture, XXXII.
87. Architecture, XXXIII.
88. Architecture, XXXIV.
89. Architecture, XXXV.
90. Architecture, XXXVII.
91. Architecture, XXXVI.